Zura Shiolashvili

The Prelude of Divine Wisdom
in the Art of Aphorism

No crowned wealth will compare with
the glory attained within poverty

Zura Shiolashvili

Zura Shiolashvili

The Prelude of Divine Wisdom in the Art of Aphorism

Zura Shiolashvili Publishing

First edition 2010

Printed in Great Britain

Second edition 2014

Revised third edition 2018 (The third printing 2020)

ISBN 978-0-9565175-2-4

Printed and bound in Great Britain.

Front cover: detail of front facade: *Vanis' Gospel* © Korneli Kekelidze

Georgian National Centre of Manuscript 2018

Dedication

To my dearest dad, Givy Shiolashvili, and my brother Konstantin Shiolashvili, now both departed from this world, and my dearest mother, Medea Samkharadze.

Heavenly Waves, Levan (Shimshilashvili) Shemesh,
© Levan (Shimshilashvili) Shemesh 2012

Contents

Acknowledgements

My deep respect go to Mr. and Mrs. Keith and Mary Gwynne, who gave me the opportunity to spend time on the first edition of my book.

Special thanks also to Dr. Martin Cohen and the late Prof. Vakhtang Jordania, for their encouragement; and to Pastor Jen Mckenzie and Mr. Stanislav Stsepaniuk for their contributions, as well as the Academic David Zilpimiani and Mr. Giga Kukhaleishvili for their support.

Finally, for the fulfilment of this important project I would like to express my gratitude to Dr. Benedict Young for his assistance in editing my writings.

Preface

Nietzsche's spirituality starts with his carnal self and ends in psychological delusion. Armed with his dissatisfactory literary art, Nietzsche must march on with a *will to power* ('master morality') that is nothing but a monster's voice within him. What could the art of his philosophy be about, after all? Merging animalistic caprice with beauty, in his 'revaluation of all values?' But is not the spirit of a beautiful soul, with its longing for the ideal, mightier than the *will to power?* The phenomenon of Nietzsche is, in fact, another testimony of the evil that dwells within *free will* as conceived by human naturalism, while implicitly acknowledging the language of truth in the Christian religion.

In Nietzsche's moral psychology, suspended between the human and the non-human, there exists only an animal disposition—for this is how Nietzsche uses the degraded spirituality to mock Christianity. In the fallen state of his consciousness, Nietzsche attempts to apply conditional logic to feelings, relying on the instinctive *will* of human nature to be deluded by empirical science.

For Nietzsche, depravity represents not psychological degradation, but rather the truth of the *free spirit.* Hence, to Nietzsche's mind, spiritual virtue lies in the fleshly nature of man. But perhaps the reality is that, despite his philosophical finery, Nietzsche ends up resembling more a *clever idiot* than—as he imagines—a knight in shining armour tasked with saving all humanity.

That which is not planted in the soul by the sacred will be washed away by futility.

If Nietzsche had known that he would be laid bare and made a laughing stock, he would have fallen on bended knees and begun to pray.

As a bibliographical note, this book is based on the previous editions of my *The Art of Aphorism and Nietzsche's Blind Passion*, now amended for a clearer and more genuine revelation of their spirit, and here republished under the title:

The Prelude of Divine Wisdom in the Art of Aphorism.

Summary

The critical introduction of the latest collection of Nietzsche's previously unpublished *Writings from the Late Notebooks*[1] casts light on the contradictions within Nietzsche's system of morality, while supporting the value of his thought. *That thought*, according to the introduction, is centred in Nietzsche's theory of man's *will to power*, a theory which ultimately fails. Also discussed is the relation of this *will to power* with the aims and ends of human existence, and with the idea that life is more than mere existence. In Nietzsche's view, "One must understand all motion, all 'appearances,' all 'laws,' as simply symptoms of inner events." The corollary of this, according to the editor:

> The difference between the organic and inorganic world is superficial, since it does not touch on the inner sources of things happening. Thus all motion, organic or not, has an inner side; and once it is established that in the organic world this inner side is the will to power, it may seem a small step to claim that it is will to power is all that happens. The somewhat cavalier fashion in which Nietzsche proceeds here, may be explained by the fact that in this point he is following his "great teacher Schopenhauer" [Nietzsche, Genealogy of Morals, Preface 5] who was quite as swift to claim that "it is one and the same will that manifests itself both in the forces of inorganic and the forms of organic nature." As far as its scope is concerned, Nietzsche's will to power simply takes over the place of Schopenhauer's "will." The great defect of the present reading is that, understood this way, the doctrine of the will to power has no chance of being true. (Bittner, "Introduction," *Writings from the Late Notebooks*, p. xxi)

If we accept Nietzsche's claim that all motion is merely symptomatic of inner events, entailing that their motion has no synchronic connection with the outside world, then how can such motions exist? But if he means that both organic and inorganic motion has an inner side, then Nietzsche is forced to admit the importance of the metaphysical world in the human spirit, which contradicts his final claims to 'wisdom.' In the introduction, the editor also very clearly notes Nietzsche's moral judgment upon Christianity and nature itself.

> As the naturalist reminds us, we are primarily living creatures; because it is hostile to life, our morality is thus a negation of our very being. Hence, we should try to liberate ourselves from it. Yet it is difficult to understand how there can be such a thing as a morality hostile to life. If we had received our morality from above, it might easily clash with how we live. In Nietzsche's view, however, our morality arises from the way we live—so how can it turn against it? (Ibid., p. xxxii)

---

[1]   Cambridge University Press 2003, edited by Rüdiger Bittner.

Nietzsche's philosophical psychology states the absolute priority of animal desire over the sublime value of mind. Seen from another perspective, this is a case of *instinctive substantiation in the animal nature,* whereby the *highest* is abandoned and the *lowest* takes its place and this *lowest* becomes the *highest* in its *pleasurable freedom.* Following his teacher Schopenhauer, *free will* for Nietzsche is no more than the means whereby a human's consciousness functions as a tool for feeling. That is, there is no autonomous metaphysical passion in the mind by which feeling can be exalted and beautified.

In short, Nietzsche holds that the mind should be driven by sense perception and its natural instinct, and that this is what talk of the human *free spirit* really portends. Hence, for Nietzsche, the idealization of animal nature in the human being represents the highest achievement for our existence. But the question is: how does Nietzsche understand animal nature in the human ego and human nature in the animal ego? It is Nietzsche's disrespectful attitude towards morality and aesthetics that requires a response, not merely the inferences he draws from this premise. Nietzsche's doctrine expresses the outlook that the goal of moral philosophy should be to displace a true understanding of the human spirit. I hope to shed some light on the ugliness of this conception of moral and aesthetic pleasure.

Scientifically, it is possible to extract a drop of blood to measure its condition
and make a diagnosis of health. Similarly, in a spiritual way,
I intend to examine some thoughts from this latest offering of Nietzsche's
writings and previous works to reveal the sensitive delusion
within his purported philosophical wisdom.

Introduction

This book's primary aim is to provide a description of the divine psychology that is present in human nature, understood in the sense of the art of comprension, from philosophical, religious and theological perspectives. Hence the nature of thinking and understanding is the main object of my writings, and I seek to bridge spiritual knowledge and the human senses in relation to the eternal nature of thought, which is the mirror of the human soul. In the main, the work contests Nietzsche's one-sided and hypocritical wisdom as regards the phenomenology of the mind and spiritual aesthetics. From a philosophical and theological standpoint, I illustrate Christian psychology as the pure beauty of spiritual and physical feelings within personal consciousness, from which faith in God is kindled. As for Nietzsche's philosophical wisdom in his 'revaluation of all values' everything is enlivened by natural instincts which are perceived inchoately through the senses; the provisional mutable character of the truth he peddles ultimately reduces them to lies. With his naturalism, and *free spirit* Nietzsche's philosophical notion of the 'death of God' gets the relationship of mind to matter upside-down; little wonder then that spiritual values are subsequently cast out from the heights to join Nietzsche down in the mud.

The project also has broader resonance, in its exploration of psychological arguments relating to spiritual understanding in the works of Freud and Jung, insofar as they refer to Nietzsche. The primary argument here is that, by locating the naturalistic urges proper to our animal background within human nature, Freud and Nietzsche deprive *the mind* of any means of regenerating, within the divine, that which represents the real sensation of beauty. In other words, we face a choice: either animality, unfolding within the natural freedom of worldly intuition; or pure humanity, as revealed in the concept of the divine within the immortality of the soul. In this contrast, my goal is to exhibit the spiritual power of sheer beauty in the world of Christ.

Hence, it is necessary to pose the question once again: Does *Christian morality* represent *slavery*, as Nietzsche claims; or is it in fact the *free spirit* which he posits in his 'revaluation of all values' that drags us into spiritual bondage? We need to see this aesthetically too. Despite the cleavage between the physical and spiritual worlds, both derive their existence from our unitary body; their confrontation in respect of human happiness is made inevitable by their contrasting natures. Nevertheless, Nietzsche understood such divergence to be a human construct that runs contrary to our natural makeup.

Accordingly, a central aspect of his philosophical project is the attempt to reunite these two aspects of the self in one single animal disposition. Nietzsche, a professor of philology, himself appears as the most impassioned Antichrist of the nineteenth century. His first spiritual teacher Schopenhauer, casts a shadow over many of his ideas: despite Nietzsche's repeated later rejections of him, his philosophy became more animal as his intellectual mastery grew.

To live alone you need to be either an animal or a god—says Aristotle.
But he left out the third case: you can be both—*a philosopher.*
(Nietzsche, *Twilight of the Idols*, p. 156, §3)

One thing is not clear here: how can an animal be *a philosopher* when its entire disposition is dedicated to *eating, drinking* and *copulation?*

I cannot move on without a short response both to Kant's transcendental aesthetic (which lacks spiritual depth) and Schopenhauer's intellectual confusion. —Both philosophically and psychologically, Christian faith is viewed by many of its opponents as an obsessive conviction, rather than the revelation of true beauty in divine mystery. In Nietzsche's case, empirical wisdom is directed just towards animal nature—a common ruse by which the vain but sensitive individual lays claims to all existence as his own inheritance, while at the same time reducing it to mere baubles of erudition, encircled by the void. In his blind glee, Nietzsche's whole life is but the reflection of the abyss wherein he gazes, an abyss which deceives him that his spiritual fall is in truth the attainment of new heights.

Nietzsche's favourite literary ingredients have always been such words as *slavery, ugliness, depravity, degradation, gloominess, degeneration, anti-nature, idiotic, etc.,* by means of which he expressed his thoughts on the Christian religion and the existence of God. Alas, with my acquaintance with this kind of philosophy, I had no alternative but to extend my hospitality to Nietzsche by serving him his own favourite dishes for spiritual nourishment. The first point that needs to be clarified is as follows: Nietzsche's psychological estimation of spiritual principles is rooted in biology, rather than the spirit we recognize as stemming from the supernature of the Deity.

I consist of body and soul—in the worlds of a child. And why shouldn't we speak like children? But the enlightened, the knowledgeable would say: I am body through and through, nothing more; and the soul is just a word for something on the body.
(Nietzsche, *Thus Spoke Zarathustra,* xxx)

For Nietzsche, it would seem that the human spirit must be subordinate to the appetence of animal nature; he considers it impossible that the animal nature could bow to the human spirit in its height. This psychological move is his fundamental tactic for destroying supremacy of thought and seeking the regression of the spiritual self. It was indeed an extraordinary theory that Nietzsche required, capable to affirm that the only truth of paradise is derived from the earth, oppose the metaphysics of the Christian religion, and synchronize the idea of eternity in the natural disposition of animal passion. This theory was his imaginary metapsychology concerning the notion of 'eternal recurrence.'

And there will be nothing new in it, but every pain and every joy and every thought and sigh and everything unutterably small and significant in your life will have to return to you, all in the same succession and sequence. (Nietzsche, *The Gay Science*, IV, p. 341)

Both the passion of the animal ego and the concept of eternity in Nietzsche's judgment are aspects of a single truth, represented in his philosophical credo. In the verbal whirlwind of his thoughts, his presumptions become a sheer delusion, but this fact remains obscured by his use of the intrinsic psychological concept of the *will to live*. There is no indispensable edification of the *pure mind* to be seen in Nietzsche's philosophy, as he is entirely naturalistically gloomy in his perception of the psychoanalysis of the soul and its immortal nature. In reality, his impassioned empiricism proposes a self-governing animal nature within a human, enslaving the spiritual consciousness to the only appetite of naural instincts which, being merely biological in their happiness, are caught in a web of the materialistic hollowness and in themselves cannot be cognizant of the truth of the mind.

Nietzsche's ideas of *free will* and self-determination are thus emancipated from the deeper morality which has in fact, inspired his polluted aesthetics and visceral version of philosophy. His phenomenology expresses a unique blend of a wicked self who has ascended to the heights of intellectual oratory, and desire to press this skill into the service of the of the Antichrist—a sight which becomes ever more worthless even as it comes to be clearer. It is therefore not surprising to find Christianity being the main target of his antagonism.

I regard Christianity as the most disastrous lie of seduction there has ever been, as the great unholy lie. I draw its aftergrowth and tendrils of ideal out from under all other disguises; I resist all half and three-quarter positions towards it —there must be war against it. (Nietzsche, *Writings from the Late Notebooks*, p. 191)

To put it briefly: in his educated guesses regarding the psychology of the animal nature of man, Nietzsche can be regarded as a great satirist of reality, for whom eternal spiritual values are a hostile intruder within his animal monism. As knowledgeable as Nietzsche was, his spiritual ignorance was twice as profound. In this book I unveil the spiritual gloom that characterizes Nietzsche's meditations, demonstrating the process by which he became a rationally polluted animal. What is the passion of life? How can it be see through the comprehension of *mind* and *body* in the personality? Is it possible to perceive the highest spiritual values without knowledge of the nature of Christ?

This is what I seek to depict in the pages that follow. Finally, all my arguments presuppose the orthodox path of the Christian religion, which I portray through a series of my aphorisms and metaphors, expressing a philosophical theology based on the spiritual aesthetics, which can be described as the science of the soul as well.

Ten Commandments, Levan (Shimshilashvili) Shemesh,
© Levan (Shimshilashvili) Shemesh 1989

Jeremiah, Simon Roman Kriheli, © Simon Roman Kriheli 2019

Chapter 1

Nietzsche's Animal Psychology and Cognitive Arguments Reflected through the Mirror of Christian Morality and Aesthetics

Gelati Gospel, © National Agency for Cultural Heritage
Preservation of Georgia 2010

Let me begin with a quote from Nietzsche that demonstrates how he perverts the notion of beauty with his naturalism.

The animal functions are, after all, in principle a million times more important than all beautiful states and heights of consciousness: these are a surplus, except where they have to be tools for the animal functions. (Nietzsche, *Writings from the Late Notebooks*, p. 214)

From this leak, we have no alternative but to think that Nietzsche's aesthetics, as expressed in *The Birth of Tragedy* and *Thus Spoke Zarathustra*, was motivated and developed entirely by his animal functions. Yet this would actually mean that Nietzsche's own consciousness was only an external decoration to be used for lure, possessing no true worth with which the value of beauty can be independently comprehended. That is, all the excellence of Nietzsche's articulateness has been dedicated to the exultation of the animal identity so as to enslave the *mind*. In brief, according to Nietzsche, *the more animalistic a human is, the more profound* its aesthetic comprehension in nature. However, if his real self is equivalent to the animal functions and not the *nature of mind*, neither his thoughts nor his animal passions can be a criterion by which to judge truth or falsity. For it is by *the pure rational mind* that a human being is seen to human, and not merely by the animal functions.

1. It is pure thought that beautifies a human being. (Shiolashvili, *Aphorisms*, p. 8)[2]

The impression of bright beauty strewn with stars does not need to be personified in a biological organism but is the true shape of a celestial body glittering in the sky. Such luminosity, as well as the beauty of wild nature painted by magic colours, has a real, pure cognitive influence on the human psyche. Therefore, we are asserting the external genuineness of a loveliness contained within cognition, which is surrounded by a universe that is not sensual, nevertheless penetrates through the consciousness to our animal ego.

Hence this means that even in our animal selves, the *faculty of spirit* is attracted to, and delighted by, the pure shapes and colours of the aesthetics of nature which it contacts via the human senses. Such linking reaffirms the existence of inner purity within human feelings. Because *an animal* is not inclined to the meaning of purity, and here we can agree with Nietzsche's claim that:

"The spirit" appears as a symptom of precisely the relative imperfection of the organism..."Pure spirit" is a pure stupidity. (Nietzsche, *The Antichrist*, p. 12 §14)

---

[2] All consecutively numbered aphorisms that appear hereafter are from this source, unless specified otherwise.

As to humans, in their pure sublime nature, we have to conclude that the existence of the self within the mind (as our second nature) is related to its inborn purity (from the divine) linked with consciousness and our physicality, enabling us to perceive both the beauty of nature and our spiritual loveliness. For this reason, the aesthetic happiness attendant on this union of nature cannot be attained by the partiality of physical craving or instincts, as they are detached from their first reason of the essential (metaphysical) body of the divine. Nietzsche has nothing to say about this, or how the beauty of true comprehension inflects our animal ego with personal glory, because in his conception the animal self is superordinate over the true idea of beauty. The latter, however, in its divine truth, is the very attitude which beautifies the inner self of the spirit—that is, purifies it for its perfection, and enables its spiritual (the eternal body of mind) and physical regeneration, which is worth suffering. Such a process has to be the main source of the transfiguration of animal nature into the true human character, and so the creation of human beings which carry the loveliness of nature within themselves.

Our divine mastery over the human ego is what gives birth to the spark of the true understanding of beauty in our sensibility. That is the *pure feeling of mind* in our soul, which originates from the celestial body of the divine. It is this which represents the regeneration of our blind human self, so as to guide our physicality to the ideal of love and its personal glory; while in its opposed fallen naturalism, a human descends psychologically into the glamour of the thirsty animal ego. Such a spiritual fall reveals a form of happiness which is its sweetest animal desire to be like an animal through personal charm.

As for the *pure feeling of mind,* it manifests the pearl of love; and it, therefore, becomes nothing but the living death of the ego in the realm of instinctual *free will* and dissolute worldliness, the essence of life, which in its lust and pride it considers fitting for a free and rational animal to attain gratification for its *will to live.* Yet the spirit's dual spiritual and physical yearning for the ideal is precisely that which constitutes hell for a free animal ego, wherein we can see the root of Nietzsche's antagonism towards idealism and Christianity. Since sensible purity for Nietzsche is a lie, any acknowledgement of the sublime nature of the mind in the divine should entail the refutation of his conception of the *will to power,* since the latter is based on the very same animal and his personal pride on which his idea of the subconscious self is established. Consequently, trying in vain to ward off spiritual starvation in his demand on physicality, Nietzsche proclaims the psychosexual superiority of the animal functions over any and *all beautiful states and superior heights of consciousness.* Such a scheme is Nietzsche's only possible means to defend his fallen conception of 'I.' If Nietzsche had ever looked at his fallen world from the vantage of the of the highest states of beauty, he would have seen vain animal self-importance harshly illuminating the empty disaster of debasement dressed up in the robes of the *free spirit*.

Instead, Nietzsche denounces true morality as all that is metaphysically absurd, and thus idealism and Christianity as 'anti-nature'—or as I would have it, *anti-mortal nature*. From then on, the slavish obedience to animal greed destroys man's aspiration for the true values of life, the very thing by which the human being is marked out to be just that—a human being. This is the gloomy picture of the debasement of spiritual worth which emerges from Nietzsche's worldly practice: elevating the animal inclination within its partial satisfaction and denying the harmony of truth through which the physical passions arrive at their perfection to be united with the immortal world in the divine Christ. It is such an aesthetic construction united with the criterion of true feelings in Deity that can be interpreted as the *pure passion of mind*.

Nietzsche could not enter that blissful state which pure human dignity discerns when it dwells within true love, nor accept through his own *free spirit* that the suffering which attends the only route through which such a condition may be achieved; instead he preferred to live like a joyous animal dedicated to the pursuit of pleasure, shunning the misfortunes of the truly human being. Since Nietzsche's empiricism afforded no place for any *beautiful state* or *heights of consciousness*, denying as he did the metaphysical body of the divinity in such states ought to be embodied, he therefore left the highest idea of beauty stranded in empty space, with animalism remaining the only source of life in his philosophy.

It is Christianity to hate spirit, to hate pride, courage, freedom, libertinism of the spirit. (Nietzsche, *The Antichrist*, p. 18 §21)

I call Christianity the one great curse, the one great innermost corruption. (Ibid., p. 66)

The church combats the passions by cutting them off in every sense:
It never asks: how can a desire be spiritualized, beautified, deified.
(Nietzsche, Twilight of the Idols, p. 172 §1)

Faith means not wanting to know the truth. (Nietzsche, *The Antichrist*, p. 52)

2. Faith in Christ introduces purity prior to spiritual knowledge,
exposing the grandeur of love within its indefinable depth.

A Christian psychology acknowledges sublime senses within our physical nature, a spirituality that is irreconcilable with the enchantments of the carnal self and its instinctive wants. Yet, through an amalgamation of hypnotic charm and demonic reason, in its conditional and instinctual conquest, the carnal lust in its sensuality is able to appear as the *pure passion of mind* itself, and thus to exert a commanding force of deception over human nature, which strays from the essential path to the aesthetic truth through the loss of spiritual self. In such a bodily-self, depraved passion in its attraction is revealed as the heavenly bliss, and the sole stimulus for life in the human spirit—this is when the *pure feeling of mind* in the divine is rendered detached and unattainable.

Seeing that the gift of consciousness also includes the freedom of the *mind*, and not only the freedom desired by the animal sensitive self, the yearning for happiness inspirits an inner tension between the value of comprehension and animal instinct for freedom. Because sensual craving gains its physical freedom through the somatological instinct, our innate carnality is in accord with neither the truthfulness nor the honour of the conscious mind itself. That is to say, a carnal instinct in its visceral superiority cannot be elevated to any beautiful feeling, despite the sensual joy which is associated with it, but remains fallen and instinctual in its depraved truth and naturalism, using its psychosexual authority to mock and enslave any aspirations to the true beauty of the mind. At heart, in its visceral autonomy, the satisfied passion pollutes and degrades the spirit, which becomes intolerable to the *pure feeling of mind*. Due to this distortion of human sensibility, a two-faced form of contradictory happiness emerges.

In respect of spiritual truth, the human senses ought to embody pure reason and its pure yearning for love, revealed as a vivid and beautiful treasure within the inner self. That is, pure rational attraction should comprise a form of satisfaction which is prior to physical glamour, avoiding pollution of the soul and pursuing the glory of loveliness in the divine. And so, it is that, in striving to conform to the greatness of love, a carnal instinct becomes abandoned from the superiority of its depraved happiness; thus in its suffering, the *breath of feeling* is captured by the transcendental loveliness and comes to reside in the divine world. In the world of Christ, the art of such a mystical performance is that it breathes sensibility into a super-personal love, with fleshly distress being transfigured and reborn into the *eternal feeling of beauty*.

As it emerges into the realm of our senses, the nature of pure thought growing in Christian psychology illuminates the human spirit in harmony with spiritual and physical love within the greatness of the eternal self, since its passion has been yielded from the *pure feeling of mind* of the divine nature. In contrast to the role played by the carnal self within the human spirit, *pure feeling* possesses an inherent freedom, and the ego, in becoming dimly aware of this realm which transcends it, naturally tends to become abusive due to its worldly freedom and self-admiration. This is because human feeling, having a merely instinctual kind of *free will*, is incompatible with the dominion of the pure *feeing of mind*, and experiences both spiritual and physical suffering as a consequence. The supernatural loveliness of sensible truth becomes attractive at only the point when human sensibility becomes embodied within the super-nature of Christ. Such a definition points towards the transcendental psychology of an immortal supersensibility by indicating the spiritual body that dwells in the Deity.

3. The invisible mountain of love makes visible the peak of beauty.

4. Can an animal be an idiot? Scientifically, no: but philosophically it is indeed possible.

5. Love is not only a sensuality but also an understanding that ought to be pure. (O, the happier animals are, the more they can live without it.).

What is Jewish morality? What is Christian morality?
Chance robbed of its innocence; happiness polluted by the concept of "sin." (Nietzsche, *The Antichrist*, p. 22)

Christianity is also opposed to everything that is spiritually well constituted—only a sick reason can be used as Christian reason, Christianity sides with everything idiotic. (Ibid., p. 51 §52)

According to Nietzsche, the concept of sin derived from a slave psychology that originated from Jewish culture, and Christianity is a branch of the same tree, causing the devaluation of happiness.

Christian spirituality is to him an ugly road of sorrow by which mankind became wretched and fearful in its hopes for mercy. Though Nietzsche was very indulgent towards 'animals,' in his hypocrisy he overlooked the simple truth that, despite their having no religion, they nevertheless have their characters: among them are both the *strong* and *weak*. This is due not to religion or faith, but to nature itself. *A deer* can never become *a wolf*, or *an ass a deer*. If a guiltless rabbit is chicken-hearted and weak, this does not mean it should be despised, but instead loved all the more. It is this that represents a genuine love of the earth, one which 'the higher man,' as Nietzsche's representative of the highest wisdom in his book *Thus Spoke Zarathustra*, was unable to see at all but on the contrary, he mocked it in relation to human beings. In this fashion, Nietzsche became a killer of even his favourite aesthetics he always relied on so extensively. Though, historically, the authority of the Christian church was corrupted, thereby causing the spiritual degradation of divine faith, the cognitive senses of divine faith on which Christianity is based are nonetheless true. So, none can oppose Nietzsche in this way, even now, many materialists with their 'will to power' and 'corrupted pleasure' can be found in the Church, yet this should not be inferred as mixing pure and impure water in the same glass. If dust covers a treasure this not does mean it should be discarded; rather, to see its worth it must be cleaned.

The existence of the mind within the body provokes an internal resistance which arises out of human nature itself, not just for religious reasons, but primarily because of thought, which discloses man's self as being rooted in the realm of the spirit. The *deeper* our spiritual and mental discernment, the *greater* suffering within our animal and human nature. This is a self-evident truth and needs no specific affirmation philosophically or psychologically.

The concept of sin is nothing but poison to the animal psyche: the physical perception of spiritual beauty infuriates its natural freedom, by intimating a disaster to its ego. Because of this, the human psyche can never by its own *free will* reject its penchant for visceral desires, since through human nature it is physicality embodied in the animal identity alone. Accordingly, Nietzsche's animality and *free will*, like all his similar cultural achievements, defile the value of the inner beauty, and in his psychosexual wisdom, he appears to mutilate his own art. Even with the excellence of stylistic form in his Zarathustra's writings, it has to be accredited that his spiritual sensibility is divested of the essential nature of mind. In his philosophy, spoken wisdom is like an attractive but unfaithful woman, and his eloquent prose is merely the decorated frame of a sullied painting, which principally displays the short-lived happiness of an earthly paradise that grows thereafter in falsehood. Hence, Nietzsche's blind-laughter portends something worse than misfortune. Though his ideas often claim to describe reality, they simultaneously reveal a misleading, individual craving that would benefit from the light of day. Take, for example, his concept of the *will to power,* which never attained its true essence—the power of the *pure word of truth*, that is, the *power of true beauty*, by which you can reign over your own paradise.

The psychological relation of the *will to power* with human genetics, as observed by Nietzsche, involuntarily returns us to the research of Biblical Genesis, when Adam was given dominion over the earth—from whence precisely this *will* stems unconsciously, thus relating to a divine order. That is, spiritually the *will to power* derives from the eternal nature of the divine we are obliged to follow in its footsteps because of the immortality of the soul. But in Nietzsche's case, we see the instinctive drive of the animal nature to get the power emanating from the human Fall under its own will.

Hence, as the *will to power* is in intrinsic of human arrogance, the craving towards it either for survival or for well-being necessitates *its spiritualization*, which is the most important characteristic value for the regeneration of the human spirit. If Nietzsche had said the *will to power* must proceed from the sublime world of mind, due to its pure virtue and beauty, he would have been nearer the spiritual truth, philosophically and psychologically. Such a mind creates a human nature which is superior to one grounded in animal power and passion alone—namely, one which, purely aesthetically transcends the animal self and its physical reasons grounded in its search for happiness. We are honoured by the very existence of our ethical and spiritual dignity to see human nature this way. The higher the purity of mind, the more freedom of the animal ego is confined. It is through *the higher purity of spirit* that a human's soul is adorned with the sensation of inner beauty drawn from the divine. In such a way, passion shares its *free will* with the metaphysical body of pure consciousness in the supremacy of heavenly love. In rejecting this conception, Nietzsche allows himself to consider Christians as nothing but domestic animals and to see 'sin' as a slave psychology, the devalued residue of Jewish culture. And surely here we could agree with him: there exists no sin for animals; they are free from it. It really would be inhuman to restrict their joyous freedom given by nature!

6. Swine are honoured with the most freedom among slaves.

When animal freedom descends into the dirt, it becomes absolute freedom, but only for swine, which are enslaved by private instincts which both constitute and define the limits of their freedom.

7. The greater the love in a heart, the holier it is—thus that which is sacred is true.

Thus, the holy cognition of the Word (logos) in Christianity serves as the pure love of the body. And the sublime concept of pure thought separated from the *free will* of animal self becomes a genuine, true humanity in the supernature of God, and beautiful in itself. Such beauty embodies the pure essence of physical attraction that can be accepted as the universal approach to love, as it is derived from the original idea of inner beauty, relating to the *pure feeling of mind* in the nature of Christ. *This is pure inspiration in the divinity of Christ and thus possessed of unalterable celestial brilliance, from the treasure of whose happiness the eternal 'I' of the personality is being perceived—that is to say, the drunkenness of everlasting happiness.*

On this basis, we may reach a conclusion to our prior line of thought: specifically that the merging of pure human sense with the supernature of Christ personifies true love. Otherwise, the human condition remains enchanted by a fallen ego, separated from the spiritual awe which is due the virtue of pure beauty, and instead loathing it through base human pride. Hence, *that which is pure in action is true, both in the notion and passion of love.*

When the instinct of life compels us to act, pleasure proves that the act is right. (Nietzsche, *The Antichrist*, p. 10 §11)

Feeling, then, in fact many ways of feeling, must be recognized as an ingredient of the will, and so, secondly, must thinking. (Nietzsche, *Writings from the Late Notebooks*, p. 36)

THE PRELUDE OF DIVINE WISDOM IN THE ART OF APHORISM

Christianity has been the worst thing to happen to humanity so far. (Nietzsche, *The Antichrist*, p. 51)

8. Arguing with a jackass should not be seen as stupidity—it is merely another great misfortune upon your head in times of disaster.

Mostly, Nietzsche's observations are full of spiritual defects. In his hedonistic wisdom Nietzsche exposes the disharmony in his psychophysical drive and thereby falls back into a hopeless empiricism. Nietzsche's spiritual growth is oriented towards the nature of feelings, through which is determined the priority of thinking—this is his simple-minded depth.

Nietzsche's existentialist heedless is completely overwhelmed and blind by his shallowness. If the life instinct compels someone to an act that he knows beforehand will express his drive for pleasure, regardless of his definition of the *mind* or of good and evil, then does man's naturalism not kindle the spark of the selfish superiority complex, turning him step by step into a rational brute, or even evil? Very wise?! If we conceive of aesthetics without spiritual beauty, can the sensible nature of man regenerate itself out of the instincts of physical pleasure? Whatever else may be said, the hedonistic cloud of Nietzsche's biological naturalism appears in the clear sky alongside Freud's psychoanalysis, morally supporting the supremacy of his theory of the *pleasure principle*. This is, in fact, the worst disaster to happen to humanity so far, since the instincts of biological and psychological needs have given priority to pleasure over the course of *true thought* and the *spiritual self.*

9. Pleasure in human physicality not only discloses loveliness but ugliness as well.

10. An animal does not suffer animalism because it is an animal, but the human has to.

Is this not reality? Indeed, nothing can be idealistic or pure for a rational brute, as its entire empirical experience is rooted only in the biophysiological instincts of the animal body, as it has no *mind.*

A scientific observation related to Nietzsche's animal self within the realm of art can be elaborated as follows. One of Freud's ideas is that all art and literature is the result of the artist's sublimation of libidinous urges. Developing Freud's idea, might we be persuaded that a sexually active man would be more inclined towards art? Even the admirable example of Nietzsche cannot cover up Freud's psychoanalytical blunder.

Freud's study of the sublimation of the libidinous urge in artists describes only the lowest stage of artistic expression, and consequently remains incomplete and therefore erroneous. Its limitation lies in its failure to account for the mastering of the psychological idea of everlasting beauty in conscious perception. But if an artist is driven by the sublimation of libidinous urges to express his sensations, he has been given a merely subjective and emotional standard—that is, a natural illusion—of universal greatness on which to base his ideal, which thus remains always trivial and eroded. It is the same artistic sensitivity that spiritually robs a person of their entire life, through illusive sensations of *superficial deepness*, which leave them trapped in the inner void of deceptive greatness and luxury.

11. Emptiness attracts the most significant income in this world.

Even in Maslow's hierarchy of needs, while aesthetic needs are linked to physiological needs, they are distanced from them, with the latter seen as lower. In Maslow's statement, an advanced level can only be reached when the previous level of needs has been fulfilled. This means that, after the biological and physiological requirements, new higher needs emerge which I would call the metaphysical chain of the next stage, that is, freedom from the previous instinctual demand. Freud himself acknowledged the double inclination of the sexual drive: arising from the visceral instincts and from the human psyche itself. Unfortunately, Freud had insufficient knowledge to spiritualize his psychoanalytic observation of the connection between artistic accentuation and sublimation urges, which means being free of the dependence on the sublimation of libidinous urges so as to release the brainchild. Otherwise, we have no alternative but to accept that all masterpieces that have ever been created were dependent on the libidinous urges of artists.

In other words, the ideal of art itself represents the instinct of libidinous urges! Freud's psychoanalysis thus brought a very noxious virus into existence. Moreover, if we accept Freud's ideas regarding the libidinous urges in artists, all sexually dissolute man in their lewdness could be called artists, save for the accident that they may not possess a paintbrush.

12. *Psychobiology* and *psychophysiology* alike characterize the instrument of an artist. While the mind of a creator is impulsively interlaced with the resonating of their strings, it will always be surrounded by provisional and illusory sensations of true feelings, which are naturally mingled with the composition of beautiful harmony just through their emotional sense perception. As a consequence, even in its imaginative acknowledgement, the spirit of an artist always remains unrelated to the *beauty* of the *eternal depths of true feelings*. To present one's true ideal oeuvre for a mind is therefore to abandon the living world wherein it has been impulsively interlaced, and master its creation by transfiguring its instrumental faculty into the sublime nature of the *pure feeling of mind*. This is the phase when an artist universally becomes a lord of his masterpiece.

This was not the result of carelessness or of lack of knowledge, but of downright resistance to the mere possibility that there could be a second psychic authority besides the ego. It seems a positive menace to the ego that its monarchy could be doubted. The religious person, on the other hand, is accustomed to the thought of not being a sole master in his own house. (Jung, *The Undiscovered Self*, p. 391)

Despite his mastery of analytical psychology, Jung was too superficial to seek to play on aesthetic strings when exploring any concept or idea of beauty. Consequently, his analysis and diagnosis cannot be aesthetically valid at all. His oratory recognizes only the physical impression of the brain, despite his topic's being suspended within the unknown inner depth of the mind.

13. Music is not just that which you listen to—it is also that which you see.

This aphorism reveals a sound of beauty unseen by Freudians in their empirical and limited psychology of aesthetic knowledge, and wholly denied in Nietzsche's philosophy. Its expression is not provoked by the sublimation of libidinous urges, but by the sublime nature of *pure feeling of thought* existing in the spirit and consciousness. On this depends not only the true essence of creativity, but also the way of truth towards Deity.

All this signifies the independence of spiritual inspiration in mind. What is the origin of this autonomy?—Is this not another hierarchical aspect of the spirit that requires respect and care under the guide of biopsychological measures? It cannot only be related to the biopsychological perspective of energy, as it is free from its natural appetite in its independent ambition: this brings to light the existence of a non-biological substance within it as well.

With it, the pure impulse in the human soul itself discloses its existence, revealed in the categorical aspirations to beauty through the transcendental nature of the divine. Hence, the mind's ability to resist the blind charm, or to exclude it from its moral frame, already represents a shift from one condition to another. This is, therefore, sufficient ground for a dualist ontology.

14. If you wish to see a miracle look at the sky strewn with stars and believe.

Man has not been created stooping towards the earth, like the irrational animals; but his body form, erect and looking heavenward, admonishes him to mind the things that are above. (Augustine, *City of God,* XXII, 24)

Another of Freud's psychoanalytical errors was his basing of broad, sweeping conclusions on his study of sexual deviations.

The sexual instinct has to struggle against various mental resistances. (Snowden, *Teach Yourself Freud*, p. 96)

It needs to be understood that sexual instincts make physiological demands upon the mind. Hence, if the psychological self is entirely derived from the sexual instinct, then what is the difference between a rational and irrational animal? The dignity of spiritual consciousness, whereby humanity is distinctive from animal nature for rational love of spiritual beauty, is omitted entirely.

The blocking of sexual instincts awakens neurotic symptoms and damages the psyche, demolishing the nature of man; the actualization of organic functions is the way to maintain a healthy constitution for the natural balance of the psyche rooted in pleasure. (Snowden, *Teach Yourself Freud*, p. 96)

Christian psychology does not evade the neurobiological aspects of pleasure but considers them through its divine principles for a clear perception of the true meaning of life. For example, the physiological maturation of physical aptitudes and pleasure rush onwards towards sensible love—they are not frequently united. Consequently, through its physicality, the bodily self consciousness pollutes the inner beauty of its feeling with dissoluteness, which is seen as a sin—not as healthy or normal. In the psychogenesis of Christianity, the conjunction between the physical and theological bodies is accomplished by the spiritual passion of the pure word and morality.

Christian psychology, (the supernatural topic of the spirit), requires physical involvement in human nature through suffering and patience, which, in the unavoidable cruelty of survival, changes and purifies the regime of the biophysiological mechanism under rules to the eternal world of divinity proportionate to a human being. *Through a pure psychology we develop the true connotation of human physiology.* Hence, in the Christian religion, the denial of self in one's own sensibility is seen as the way of truth within the timeless conscious beauty provided by divine elevation over the *slavish pleasure of a sin.* The latter, in its blind will, grows to be ugly and dishes up evil through its polluted freedom.

An ontological evolution is experienced within the Christian world, which countenances a transfiguration of animal psychology into a complete, pure sensibility, with the divine world thereby becoming perceptible. In this manner, the natural state of the psyche becomes spiritually and unconditionally intoxicated with the super-sensitive beauty of the *heavenly kingdom of God.*

15. Longing surpasses the unattainable.

And if your eye causes you to sin, pluck it out and throw it away; it is better for you to enter life with one eye than with two eyes be thrown into the fire of hell. (Matthew, 18: 9)

The significance of the injunction in the Book of Matthew has to do with the curtailing and rejection of our worldly inclination that separates us from the divine beauty. Christ is speaking, apropos of our sensory world, of that which triggers transgression in our physical actions. Taken literally, if we pluck out our eyes, yet our sensory desire for sin remains within us, what meaning does this rejection bear? To reiterate, the animal nature in man is not itself equal to a demonic will, but the diabolical will acts in the animal nature of a human, in human nature and all along life itself; in times of human sorrow as well as happiness—appearing as a saviour (an angel) in our fallen sensibility and self-indulgence. Naturally, evil invites a man to the desired joy and luxury, helping him overcome all obstacles through resort to anti-divine actions, and ultimately then to bow to Antichrist as the prince of this world. Evil, in its worship of its own materialistic self-glory and appetite for depraved sensation, loathes the eternal depths of truth, and thieves from it in order to debase that which is truly beautiful and eternal; this it does entirely for its own demonic mesmerism, through which in the Worldly Nature it has learned to prosper.

Back to Freud.

'Sexual satisfaction:' the very term is corruptive and denies the existence of spiritual depth, relating only to the animal nature of the human and not the human soul itself. What is the main spiritual motivation for this physical pleasure? What underlies its satisfaction? In Freud's naturalism, we encounter real psychological trouble, which involves the physiological. And yet, we may ask —does *free will* exist, located in the psychogenesis of a person between the comprehension of self and the sensation of pleasure, or is this *free will* itself a masquerade for the fulfilment of natural violence? The absence of the divine manifested in love impoverishes the human soul. Man, thus wishes to elude the inner emptiness of his happiness by seeking a 'compulsory vitalization' through the lower disposition of his instincts, namely the blind sexual drive to which the human self is attracted in those instants of excitement that are detached from the true feelings of the inner self. This then gives birth all over again to the sense of sensual hunger within the human ego, for the feeling of happiness has been driven out of the disposition to bodily arousal which occurs in carnal partiality, and its depraved touch manifests as the lower bodily self for personal adulation through hidden pleasure; the latter then in those instants acts as a partial guide for the higher self, yet evil by its very nature is camouflaged therein. This is to say, it seeks for a moment to lay hold of its own partial sense of enchantment, by adopting a stance of *vivifying astonishment* in the face of the *eternal breath of passion within itself* (as it is called, 'sexual satisfaction'), where this is veiled by Mother Nature as the realm of mere happiness and as, the essence of all loveliness. To all appearances, in its dualistic revelation, this is a sure means towards the dissipation of psychological sensibility in the search for love and pleasure within human *free will*. So it can and should be argued that the *everlasting breath of passion* is one of the leading psychological factors, differentiating humans from animals in the activity of lust, by which man satisfies his rational greatness. This was partially analysed by Freud as 'the energy of life' in the sexual instinct, without offering any observations in his psychoanalysis as regards the genesis and the real essence of this energy, the substance of which is based on the *eternal breath of passion* within it itself, conducted by the unconscious mind through the nervous system, the sensation of which cannot conceivably spring from the substance of mortal nature, either *organically* or *meaningfully*.

Since *pleasure* in itself discloses within the psyche a momentary hope of timeless existence, the human spirit absorbs the impression of its truth with great wonder, celebrating both physically and spiritually its mesmerizing perfection. Even though this *everlasting breath of passion* is depraved and delusive in its bodily glamour, the mortal nature of man, which instinctively seeks spiritual and physical vitality in self-gratification, becomes pleased with empirical possession in the hope of finding heavenly paradise (the divine energy) in whatever it is charmed by. This is of a piece with momentarily throwing the burden of living into the abyss of the past, yet afterwards inevitably with a fresh stimulus to resume the battle for life's desired goal and happiness.

It stands to reason that a human's personal goal, and its yearning for it, is vivified by a sense of the *eternal* within the subconscious. It is a natural disposition for the human being to be instinctively attached to pleasure by an intuition arising from its biopsychological demands, motivated by the *will to an eternity* that is non-existent in time. It is sensible to say that the *everlasting ethos of the soul* was over time deformed and transformed into biological science; and it was the biopsychological instinct of pleasure in the time, stripped of its eternal spiritual core, that was canonized by Freud as the *pleasure principle*. To compare accurate impressions with the delusive side of passions— that is, the theory of the *pleasure principle* —and to see eye-to-eye with the theological, is to affirm that the spiritual attitude (the pure nature of mind) relates to the bodily structure via the physical *will*. This means that the physical *will* is not totally controlled by the organic body, and if it does come to be so controlled, then this has to be seen as the act of either a purely animalistic or openly evil being. Without doubt, the physical instinct considered as a biopsychological aspect of human nature also has its own share of instinctive depravity. What does a human being receive, and what are the final outcome for the human spirit, from the sensation of this joyful aptitude excited by depraved passion which never attains the essential gratification? *Lust itself transcends the empirical world (space-time) through intrinsic ecstasy, wherein the blind rapture finds its happiness minute in being deluded.*

16. A minute's existence in empty space equates to eternity in its duration of time.

17. The *will to* pleasure is triumphant over the obstacle existing between the human and animal natures.

As it naturally stands, pleasure is in some ways a necessary organic lie, conveying a deceptive excitement which is integral to the *will to live* as it resides in human psychology. With a similar psychological principle of pleasure for example, in his spiritual fall, the psyche of an alcoholic takes for granted his endless *breath of joy* in alcoholism: this is his personal thrill, that is, his 'heavenly feeling.' Likewise, a drug addict finds his delusive *everlasting breath of passion* in drugs. We can conclude that both spiritually and physically, the equilibrium of the psyche is to be found within the *eternal breath of passion* and its astonishing vitality, not within the scenario of pleasure itself, in both the conditional and unconditional states to which a human being is attached at every turn; through which man's spirit hunts for the inner glory of his self-perfection. From a neurophysiological perspective, it appears reasonable to propose that the fear of death or expectation of tragedy is instinctively expelled or at least minimized by drugs or alcohol, as well as by the arousal of carnal pleasure, as they summon to the psyche the mesmerizing *everlasting breath of passion*. This could be one of the main arguments for the correlation and indeed dependency between neurophysiology and the *pleasure principle*, as well as neurophysiology and ecstasy, within the human spirit. It is herein that all resistance to disaster and the feeling of mortality has triumphed within the human psyche, and herein that everything is morally and psychologically vindicated because of the sensation of the paradisal glory of the *eternal (heavenly) breath of passion,* which transcends the empirical world (space-time), and which itself, in its happiest relief is mingled with the *will to live*. The depraved sensation of the *eternal breath of passion* in its satisfaction, is one further means used by the instinct of self-preservation to overcome depression within the physiological self, yet it basically changes nothing for the regeneration of the spirit, merely prolonging a natural illusion in physical pleasure for psychological equilibrium and an instinctual vitality, which gradually leads feelings to a permanent emaciation. In such a way, a human being becomes ever more spiritually blind and superficial in its joy. This could also be a dialectical truth in Nietzsche's philosophy, whereby he tacitly acknowledged the origin of spiritual values.

The second temptation of passion is that, empirically, in the minute of pleasure the human spirit attains the *essence* of freedom. Given these sensations, it should be evident that Nietzsche accomplishes the intended idea underlying his empiricism: when the instinct of life compels us to act, pleasure proves that the act is right. It is less doubtful that the illusive *everlasting breath of passion* wthin Nietzsche's empirical aesthetics illustrates that he was also influenced by Schopenhauer's concept of the *will to live*, since unlike Schopenhauer himself, Nietzsche did not experience it from the standpoint of pure divine wisdom—

little wonder, considering his deluded biological naturalism, his mockery of the Christian religion. And indeed, both Nietzsche and Schopenhauer failed to comprehend that the *will to live* and the *highest spiritual values* are interrelated, both psychologically and spiritually, with the *supernature of beauty*. It would be unfair here to leave behind the sunny landscapes of Freud's psychoanalysis without acknowledging that he was as deluded as Nietzsche when he formulated the sexual instinct through his scientifically accurate reflections on depravity, free from any moral feeling.

As to the sexual instincts on the other hand: it is obvious that they reproduce primitive states of the living being, but the aim they strive for by every means is the union of two germ cells which are specifically differentiated. If this union does not take place germ cells die like all other elements of the multicellular organism. Only on this condition can the sexual function prolong life and lend it the semblance of immortality. (Freud, *Beyond the Pleasure Principle*, p. 54)

The conception of "sexuality"—and therewith that of a sexual instinct—certainly had to be extended, till it included much that did not come into the category of the function of propagation, and this led to outcry enough in a severe and superior or merely hypocritical world. (Ibid., p. 65)

The treatment of these themes, death and the duration of life among organisms, in the works of A. Weismann possesses the greatest interest for us. This investigator originated the distinction of living substance into a mortal and an immortal half; the mortal is the body in the narrower sense, the soma, which alone is subject to natural death; while the germ cells are potentially immortal, in so far as they are capable under certain favourable conditions of developing into a new individual, or expressed otherwise, of surrounding themselves with a new soma. (Ibid., pp. 56–57)

Will a Freudian psychoanalysis of the sexual instinct and immortal existence lead us to the truth? While the germ cells are potentially immortal, in so far as they are capable under certain favourable conditions of developing into a new individual, or expressed otherwise, of surrounding themselves with a new soma: might we think that the meaning of immortal existence is bound up with the sexual instinct and so is linked indirectly with depravity? In these circumstances, what kind of promises can a new individual or a new soma have of mortal life or eternal hell? But if our immortal existence is proved on the authority of biological science, which allows depravity to enter in because of the role played therein by the sexual instinct, then, it means that our morality develops our mortality (in what Freud categorizes the death instinct in its moral implications). Is it not better from Freud's point of view to be an irrational animal for our daily happiness?

Alternatively, if the moral law is embedded in immortal existence, in some agreement with organic nature that the germ cells are potentially eternal, It is uncertain why Freud expresses disquiet regarding the inhibition of the sexual instinct. Is he drawing a line between the sensual instinct and pure moral feeling, such that a man might under favourable conditions be reborn spiritually through the moral law as a new individual? That is, might a human-animal not be driven by delusive genetic instincts but perform its sensual instinct through responding to its moral feeling. In human nature, the union of two germ cells is not dependent merely on the sexual instinct of bodily psychology, but also on the aesthetics of pure consciousness; yet this latter cannot be accredited to the higher animal itself—it is the virtue of the higher man in its physicality.

Human longing for the sublime nature of happiness dispels the fear of the inevitability of death which is rooted in the subconscious. Yet can there be any truth within human sensibility based on free aspiration?

18. As pleasure in itself discloses a momentary hope of timeless existence within the psyche, a human existing in his temporal dimensions is involuntarily subjugated to the truth defined by a fleeting time. For the pursuit of rapture, with its momentary hope of timeless existence, also reveals the essence of freedom (supersensitive freedom) within itself, and, in this temporary astonishment, the spirit of a human is thereby rewarded with the fortune of ecstasy that is bound up within the feeling of super happiness. This is how the natural truth manifests itself within the temporary sensibility of a human's ego; it is precisely because its appetence is provisional that truth always remains illusive.

From these arguments, it is noticeable that all Nietzsche's philosophical aesthetics have prospered upon the basis of the same deceptive fascination of a life's happiness. On the other hand, we can state that the motivation of the endless existence revealed in delight is innate to the human psyche, and is prior to corporeal human existence, expressing the *will to live*. This shows again that *the psychology of a human, in its mortal form, is enlivened by the ethos of eternal passion, bringing into being the sense of astonishment and wonder, in which a human's craving has been rooted from the beginning of time.* Yet the real importance of this joy is the spiritual triumph, it portends over the power of evil, which is what truly enhances the significance of being.

19. If a human spirit could not experience an *everlasting passion* of joy for a moment, even through its delusive sensibility, man could not exist even for a minute.

Accordingly, it should be acknowledged that if there were not a sense of *astonishment,* the notion of spiritual longing would be no more than an irrational animal disposition. It is the sense of *astonishment,* which opens a space for the development of *mind* in our psyche both in the world of science and humanity. Hence the rational mind, being dispassionate about the yearning for *astonishment* (which is also the psychological stimulus upon which aesthetics dedepends), is the very same as the void of non-existence within sensibility, where spiritual and physical depressions are accompanied by an impression of pessimism, fear, and the feeling of death. If we attempt to comprehend spirituality through the *beginning of time* with the empirical fact of astonishment, through which evil also manipulates us with the deceitful revelation of beautiful passions, and the transcendental charm to be found in the mystery of its artistic lure but the rational 'I', in its divine purity, comes to appear as the highest feature of the spiritual aesthetics in its wonder. The pure 'I' in the word of Christ models the value of the spirit, from the biophysiological, to the sensual, to the rational, and thence to the pure spiritual self within physicality. All of these are metaphysically fettered to each other by life and death in the corporeal world; the chain of their resistance portrays both the divine and the evil sides of human character.

20. Beauty within nature is divided: when turning to dust and ashes, and when it becomes embodied within immortality.

Even if a man gives his all to his way of life and his highest goal is achieved, he falls into a sense of insufficiency if his triumph is not also crowned by the *pure feeling of mind*; his spiritual self descends into materialism, since his glory is not interrelated with the *eternal depths of divine beauty*.

21. You stand on the peak, the bottom of the precipice moves your soul even there—this is emptiness.

Nietzsche's additional advice:

"So long as men praise you, you can only be sure that you are not yet on your own true path but on someone else's."

With his limited spiritual insight, Nietzsche was unable to observe that neither praise nor disapproval can determine the way of truth, which is more important than one's own path in its mortality.

The things and properties in the sensible world are not fully real, since they are not unconditionally what they appear, since how they appear depends on a point of view. Sensible things can take on contrary properties for this reason as well if one point of view changes; the properties sensible things appear to have are therefore determined partly subjectively. (Shand, *Philosophy and Philosophers*, Plato, p. 26)

To clarify once more: if our inner world craves happiness rationally as well as sensitively, in order to imbibe aesthetic satisfaction and splendour, it does not follow that such naturalism provides us with an epistemological foundation built upon existing senses. The activity of our feelings does not substantiate the genuine *will* of our souls, other than to enforce obedience to a prior authority apprehended by fallen instincts, the behavioural reflection of which can be seen in the hedonism of human *free will* which scorns the pure ideal of love (the only true spring of the eternal). But in so doing, the greatness of the spiritual self is itself animalized through its dualistic freedom and partial instincts, and in its place the psychological unity of the mob is celebrated for the intertainment of its natural gluttony according to the *pleasure principle*.

22. The spirit of a gratified animal, however, remains empty, for its animal psyche includes no meaningful thought. Namely, the human sense dependent on physical satisfaction alone, results in desolation.

23. The nobleman is he who has experienced the spiritual bitterness within the succulent fruit of animalistic whim, and has rejected his slavish nature within it.

The only possible path to the truth within self-awareness is when aesthetic taste is defined by the spiritual 'I' in the heavenly kingdom of the divine being, and thus possesses the everlasting breath of beauty within the super-personality.

> Truly, truly, I say to you, unless one is born anew,
> he cannot see the kingdom of God. (John 3:3)

24. He who has passed through the way of death, and mastered spiritual beauty, is victorious.

25. As an animal is unable to apprehend that it is an animal, for it is an animal; likewise we are unable to perceive the sin in human pleasure, as we are sinners.

From all these considerations we can conclude that a spiritual science which proceeds without Christian spirituality imparts only blindness to man. If we remember Nietzsche's moral values, all psychological purpose focuses on what is desired by a man in his natural wilfulness, and Nietzsche's language becomes ironic in its significance on the need to acquire knowledge in order to understand what constitutes spiritual autonomy. The mark of the pleasure-seeker is displayed in a philosophy that sacrifices human virtue for the dominance of his selfish gluttony.

26. Love and faith in divinity express the eternal nature of beauty.

Of course, this is not the case for Nietzsche's empirical meditations, for here the proposition that 'God is dead' discloses Nietzsche's project as one of maniacal self-glorification rather than an expression of disbelief concerning the existence of God. For how can God die if He does not exist? But if He exists, then His death cannot be essential, as He is God. Therefore, the metaphor 'God is dead' ought to be judged a linguistic contradiction, which implicates the very heart of the Nietzschean philosophy.

The tragedy of Zarathustra is that, because his God died, Nietzsche himself became a god. (Jung, *Psychology and Religion*, p. 143)

Here Jung knocks at the right door and could still be welcomed even by Christians. Did Nietzsche's table retain any taste of the truth in his scholarly knowledge and empiricism? When no pure laws of thought can be admitted in Nietzsche's mind and aesthetics; and how can his rational principles have any virtue in his polluted coherence? Nietzsche's windy sarcasm scatters every philosophy it encounters, from the ancient Greeks to German idealism, while the Nietzschean free spirit throws down the gauntlet to the afflicted 'I' distressed by pure consciousness, which Christianity overestimates.

The origin of evil in general is to be found in the mystery of freedom (i.e. the speculative aspect of freedom) the mystery whereby freedom of necessity arises out of the natural level of the will and is something inward in compression with that level. It is this natural level of the will which comes into existence as a self-contradiction, as incompatible with its self in this opposition, so it is just this particularly of the will which later makes itself evil. (Hegel, *The Philosophy of Right*, p. 139)

According to Jung, Nietzsche's claim that 'God is dead' came, for many in Europe at the time, as a truth that allowed them psychosexually to relax their burdened psyches. In this sense, Nietzsche's claim can be acknowledged as something ordinary and practical in the monism of human psychology, rather than as a contribution to spiritual rebirth, which rationally portrays that which is *beautiful* in the understanding of life.

27. The true word in its purity is the heart of life springing from eternal breathing.

Nietzsche had no insight or understanding in his worldly truth, but only a skill in transmuting noble ideas into phantoms. For Nietzsche, *free will was* the moral vagueness of the conscious mind; the derivation of this 'will' was associated with the empirical truth of his self-awareness for the achievement of its purpose. Due to this, the instinctive *will to power* turned out to be the only guide in Nietzsche's philosophical psychology. The notion of gradualism in Darwin's theory of evolution had to be thus a mediator for Nietzsche's naturalistic doctrine and a solution to the ambiguity in his self-perfection, rather than the key to the true meaning of thought contained within this *will to power*; as a consequence, his conscious mind was left wildly disgruntled.

The criterion of truth lies in the increase of the feeling of power. (Nietzsche, *Writings from the Late Notebooks*, p. 16)

When Nietzsche realized that all his philosophical knowledge was losing its potential for the dominance of the highest of spiritual values, in his spiritual void the *will to power* converted his philosophical passion to the only hope to challenge evil. When the feeling of power in Nietzsche's philosophy is what edifies the purely impulsive model, the essential nature of mind having entirely lost its independence in his philosophy, how can it be bracketed together with the criterion of truth in its battle?—Either the chaotic power or the chaotic truth? That is to say: many truths, and many lies in their visceral rights? Can the idea of truth be conceivable without idealism or the concept of idealism without truth, if they are not debased? What kind of truth lies in Nietzsche's feeling of power? It is not the main issue here whether Nietzsche links physical and health conditions to the feeling of power. The question is: how it could be associated to the idea of truth in philosophy?

The feeling of power, as one of the leading factors in the satisfaction of ambition, has an impact on the conscious mind of humanity, blockheads included. But how can this *feeing of power* be implanted and balanced in someone's conscious mind and spirit, in the absence of wisdom or any sensibility to the ideal? Nietzsche's criterion of empirical truth is therefore doubly faked, not even acknowledging that in his philosophical vocabulary the word 'truth' is itself a linguistic illusion.

At the same time, if we follow Nietzsche's 'wise' ideology in declaring that feelings are a criterion of moral naturalism and thinking, not vice versa, it's not difficult to imagine how chaotic and dangerous the *will to power* might be which then governs the *mind*—and indeed, we don't even need description, given that we have historical examples from the middle of previous century, and elsewhere. This is a good evidence of how evil poked fun at Nietzsche.

...the will to power is the origin of justice...(Nietzsche, *Writings from the Late Notebooks*, p. 144)

28. The one who sits on a jackass and does not intend to dismount is named a jackass with a double head!

If by this observation Nietzsche intended to describe the world as it actually exists, we may well wish to agree. But how can this phrase be related to the truth in our rational understanding of it? If the *will to power* is the origin of justice, then behind this *will to power* there must be a higher wisdom or truth which endeavours to conduct this justice to the best of its ability. But without spiritual supervision, this 'will' is blind, egocentric and evil. How should we follow Nietzsche's philosophical supervision concerning this 'will' in his rational blindness?

Indisputably, we here encounter Nietzsche's psycho-philosophical distress and the spiritual failure that was the main root of his aesthetic frustration. Therefore, Nietzsche sees it, the *will to power* must appear to him as the only picture-frame for his spiritual and aesthetic truth. This thus poses the presence of power without the meaning of love. Nietzsche is a perfect example of how the greatness of a knowledgeable man can become an object of pity. So, there is little need to take a wild leap from the Christian principles concerning 'pride,' being first of the seven deadly sins, to the consequences for both understanding and action. For instance, he claims that the weak and failures should perish, we might ask more humanely: why our master morality should not instead allow them to survive?

To put the point once again, the battle between good and evil is not a separate contest of power over existence or the drive for well-being: *the thirst for victory is essential to the human spirit, enabling him to challenge the cruelty entrenched in both happiness and death.*

29. In battle with a cobweb you will not be able to annihilate the sensation of dampness itself: as for the spider enwebbed within, an illuminated corner is the fatal pillar of its rotten pleasure.

The value of truth lies not within the idea of eternal being alone, but within the infinite loveliness of the soul—or rather, it is not from being that pure beauty springs, but rather from sheer loveliness that existence springs. For mortal nature is not only rational but is also an irrational substance that cannot produce the idea of loveliness by itself, nor be blinded by that which lies beyond its substance: it can only be created within. Therefore, we have to conclude that the idea of pure loveliness is derived from beyond the mortal world—to invoke the word, from God.

30. Genuine love sheds light on indefinable beauty; pure beauty sheds light on indefinable love.

In the free spirit of Homo sapiens, there are three possibilities to obtain absolute freedom in self-realization: one ought to be a saint at heart, a complete idiot, or a rational beast!

Once self-consciousness has reduced all otherwise valid duties to emptiness and itself to the sheer inwardness of the will, it has become the potentiality of either making the absolutely universal its principle, or equally well of elevating above the universal the self-will of private particularity, taking that as its principle and realizing it through its actions, i.e., it has become potentially evil. (Hegel, *Philosophy of Right*, p. 139)

For Nietzsche, monism ploughs the hill by its own power; but is not the value of the yield more significant? This idea is too spiritual and hard to bear, yet it is more comfortable for Nietzsche to live with brutish psychology when understanding is primary defensible by existence, not when ideals justify life.

Now it is with man as with this tree. The more it wants to rise into the heights and the light, the more determinedly do its roots strive earthwards, downwards, into the darkness, into the depth—into the evil.
(Nietzsche, *Thus Spoke Zarathustra*, p. 69)

The height, which is dependent on the darkness, sustains decomposition in its existence, while growth takes place in the natural environment of purity. Nietzsche does not want to confess anything in his 'empirical naturalism'. He turns a blind eye not only to the spiritual sense of being but also to the natural involvement of wild nature in its purity which is linked with human nature as well. Nietzsche develops his rational monism through his naturalistic criterion of mortality, arguing that insofar as you are human, to that degree you ought to be an animal in your own self-development, and so be no less powerful than you are evil. This raises the question of the extent to which it is possible to develop your skills together with evil, without any inner contradiction of your senses, while remaining a man with virtue. Or do we need this kind of power and prosperity if we lose our spiritual beauty? That is another reckless aspect of Nietzsche's naturalism whereby his metaphorical identity is sustained in to the depth into the darkness—into evil, as he openly declares.

31. Life and the world would not exist without light, without darkness—neither would human beings.

Pleasure in lying as the mother of art, fear and sensuality as the mother of religion. (Nietzsche, *Writings from the Late Notebooks*, p. 144)

32. Pure awareness possesses the spiritual greatness of physical existence in the form of art.

Nietzsche's nihilistic meditation bears the imprint of a naturalist account of fallen beauty, reproducing in its representation of its object the corruption inherent within his methodology. Fundamentally, his false monism could be attached only to a psychosexual instinct in search of fleeting satisfaction, upon which his intellectual art depended: namely, on the sublimation of the libidinous urge.

33. For some, the value of a minute seems a century; for others, a century seems but a minute.

And despite his brave sensual wisdom and his deep research in the scientific arts, Nietzsche became infected with syphilis, and paralyzed.

We know that Nietzsche went to a brothel in 1865, but he claimed to have come away without touching anything except a piano. It is not impossible that, as Thomas Mann conjectures, he went back, but it is unlikely. Unless we can be quite sure that the final madness was syphilitic—and we can't—there is no need to assume that he must, somehow or other, have infected himself with syphilis…Freud and Jung helped to propagate that he contracted syphilis in a Genoese male brothel. There is no reason to think he was ever a practicing homosexual, though Freud was possibly right to explain his obsession with his own ego as homosexual and narcissistic. (Hayman, *Nietzsche*, pp. 10–11)

Physiologists argue that the lust pertaining to sexual hunger could be defined as monosemous, like the biological component of the hunger for food, which must be satisfied by any and all means. However, taking obesity into account, greed might also be causing a hunger that increases the likelihood of many diseases threatening of human life, wherefrom we cannot avoid cognitive problems relating to the psyche. Judging aesthetically, why can we not proclaim the craving for carnal lust, likewise with gluttony in hunger, as a step towards depravity as a deadly sin, where the hunger as such (the obesity), on the other hand, threatens our life? Can we not see the agreement between the epistemology of the Christian religion and the true merit of the rational mind with which we have to strive for our physical existence?

34. Because it continually searches for true pleasure, our worldly desire predestines us to be a servant to the partial feelings of their changeability, simultaneously, their rush onward towards beauty perceived by the mind. Such naturalism in its favouritism insists on its right to define the attractiveness of pleasure in its tangibility independently. So, it is this that ruins the true world of our spirituality. For the happiness defined by just an external sexual desire in our dualistic nature, is, as should be admitted, a degradation of the mind (an event unfortunately all too ordinary in the broader society of today). That is, such a definition of happiness may be said to aspire towards happiness lacking a consciousness—to try flying without wings. (Shiolashvili, *Beauty is the Guide of Happiness*, p. 115)

Slave Morality

In his habitual imperative mood, Nietzsche proclaims in *Ecce Homo,* become what you are—But by virtue of what? If the consciousness of a human self stands lower than his instinctive will, then the consciousness is secondary to the animal self. As our great Nietzsche describes it, consciousness is simply a tool. That is, the only domain of self-awareness is the animal self—what, then of the human? The simple fact is that it is not a bodily instinct but rather consciousness that formulates the structure of the personality within the human spirit, and only insofar as the bodily instinct is deprived of personality's virtue by Mother Nature, which seems not to apply in the case of Nietzsche. How then should consciousness define the true self of a person such that it is able to become what its physical character really is, when it has no room independently to determine its animal ego, and it is just a servant (a tool) to its lord (to its animal ego?). Its judgment from within will always be a slavish determination of its true self with reference to its animal self-respect. Hence a slavish judgment will permanently be associated with slave morality and the only freedom in this slavery will be the ability to satisfy the demands of its animal ego. Is this a Nietzschean *free spirit* that demonstrates the essence of freedom? A philosophy of this kind should therefore be called *a slave morality of animal freedom*—which was manipulated by Nietzsche to play the role of a *master morality* upon which has been based a significant part of modern European intellect and culture! And even once we perceive that it is upon a Nietzschean delusion that such a culture has 'thrived,' we remain unable to cast off *the salve morality of animal freedom* from the understanding of the free spirit now predominant within European thought.

...nowhere else have alcohol and Christianity—two great European narcotics—been abused with greater depravity. (Nietzsche, *Twilight of the Idols*, p. 187 §2)

The question is, how does Nietzsche—in his obscene psychology—define depravity? Can a speaking swine instruct others on the subject of dirt?

35. A blockhead can foul you as much as a swine.

Nietzsche's special attention to music displays the same logical character. No melancholy idealism or divine harmony is permitted to fracture the human joy of the mortal world. It seems, according to Nietzsche, we must ignore even the music of Bach?!

Wagner had accepted step by step everything that I hate—even anti-Semitism. (Nietzsche, *Nietzsche Contra Wagner*, p. 276)

Some of his critical notes towards Wagner's music are thus:

Beauty is tricky: let us be on guard against beauty! And particularly melody! Nothing is more dangerous than beautiful melody! Nothing is surer to ruin the taste. We will be lost, my friends, if people start liking beautiful melody again. (Nietzsche, *The Case of Wagner*, p. 6)

Nietzsche is here caught in his own trap, though he magnanimously leaves us this pearl of wisdom as a parting gift—that beauty is tricky—and ends up by baring the seductive animal insight that appears throughout his oratorical work of aesthetics. Even these words are enough to indicate that Nietzsche has converted himself into a misfortunate clown, driven by a demonic psychology which returns over and over again to his spiritual misery.

Pure spirit is a pure lie. (Nietzsche, *The Antichrist*, p. 8)

Pure spirit: the idea is too abstract for Nietzsche's mode of insight, threatening his animal wisdom mixed with his spirituality. And yet, by what means does the pure concept impact on the rational mind?

The precise result of thinking should be pure: if the analysis of precision is impure (polluted), even if it is explicit, then what value can its accuracy have? Therefore, to get a true result, we need a pure analysis of the autonomy of mind through awareness (divine faith); this should be accepted as a universal concept of judgment in our personal selves, in both the inner and outer world. This suggests the conclusion that purity is the measure of precision for the rational mind.

36. There exists no spiritual depth deprived of purity; any knowledge which contradicts it cannot be related to the true understanding of life, and its claims to have worth can be based only on polluted deception or animalistic appeal.

In the universal concept of pure psychology, the Christian religion personifies the physicality of self-comprehension in divine nature, by which the idea of love possesses pure beauty through the heavenly realm of immortality.

Within the substance of nature, purity is likewise exposed to the surrounding atmosphere by those processes that are the necessary conditions for any species to exist. So, we can conclude that the vital merit of life for existence is *purity*, both in our inner and outer worlds; and this is a purity which we are obliged to inherit. How can we separate from it in our waking life, whether we believe in God or don't? Belief in God is not blind conviction devoid of any phenomenology of the mind. It is the true mystery of the conscious mind in its physicality within the spiritual body of Christ disclosing *the eternal breath of the soul.*

37. The peak of the soul is illuminated in its immeasurable depth.

As long as the concept of truth always and everywhere remains corrupted in Nietzsche's genealogy, I would compare Nietzsche's anthropological arguments to the experience of a sailor who bears the name but does not know how to swim.

38. When you love with the whole of your heart—you touch the soul, not the body.

Sensual pleasure: innocent and free to free hearts, the earth's garden joy, an overflowing of thanks to the present from all the future. (Nietzsche, *Thus Spoke Zarathustra*, p. 207)

Sensual pleasure: the great symbolic happiness of a higher happiness and highest hope. (Ibid.)

All the allurement of Nietzsche's artistic fluency is natural, concerning the *everlasting breath of passion*, which itself is sensed by joining the present and the future, and which is seductively attached to the natural truth.

Oblivion, Simon Roman Kriheli, © Simon Roman Kriheli 2018

When the external senses of the human nature, by free will, are attracted to the prospect of excitement, they spring towards conditional feelings for their carnal satisfaction and temporary truth, which subsequently bring into effect an emptiness through which evil is able to penetrate into the human spirit. This is a consequence of a flawed happiness which desires only its carnal gratification.

Though, however, such lustful hunger reveals its attraction to be naturally true in instinctual sensibility, which at the same time contradicts and disdains the true essence of its craving and sensation within the unconditional feelings of the mind—by which we are all predestined to be duped by evil.

It should be stressed that Nietzsche's seductive impact on psychology rested on the great influence of his artistic expression, his facility with phonetic forms and phonology. But how can the correlation between these impressions, shapes and sounds convey anything semantically truthful, given that they issue from an autonomous linguistic faculty of the mind, unconditioned by the conscious self? Anyway, judging by psychological appearances, it seems that the aesthetic side of his metaphor for sensible happiness draws its inspiration from his lustful reference to the *everlasting breath of passion*. This is the 'intellectuality of feeling,' as Nietzsche names it—but do these 'intellectualities of feelings' reveal their truthful meaning in their aesthetic expression as such, as opposed to their first reason and consequences?

Now look at Nietzsche's 'intellectual feelings' from the purely analytical and aesthetic stance: Zarathustra, a symbol of the highest wisdom as depicted by Nietzsche, rewords the truth of aesthetic judgment just through reference to lust. In lustful joy and ecstatic will, Zarathustra's highest happiness is attracted to arousal by voluptuousness, which does not rise above the superficial enchantment of the bodily glamour whereby his soul is exalted in its paradisal joy.

This raises the question of how a higher happiness and highest hope can be ascribed to sensual pleasure without naturally giving rise to the supremacy of deception which is only carnal, and wherein the long-lasting *pure feeling of the inner beauty* in a person is absent in its bodily gratification? In its *free will*, the symbolic happiness linked to the ecstasy which occurs simply by sensual arousal can be filthy, ugly, and animalistic as well—affording the *same sensations* and *experience* for everyone in its own condition. Which of these can be the true impressions: all of them in all their dimensions as an expression of *a higher happiness and highest hope* according to their *innocent hearts*?

In its demonic trap and superiority, evil always captivates the human's self with the false sublime passion of paradisal joy to separate the human spirit from the heavenly kingdom of God.

39. Carnal lust is the most fabulous lie irrespective of whatever exists in man's world.

This dominant seductive glamour also contains within itself the natural bliss in which the demon released through neuroscience reigns supreme; this is a delusive paradise wherein a human can enjoy the psychosexual charm. Its lustful arousal enslaves the entire inner of world a human being, and commands us trance-like to act for our own self-satisfaction, which appears to us as the shortest route to a sublime glory in happiness that life's dream and goal has ever succeeded in rewarding. However, all happiness is destined to impoverish the *deepest passion* so long as *the true feeling of love* has been deprived of its passionate heaven and the supersensitive joy of paradise—for which everything was given, and *the true love of inner self* remains redundant.

40. It elevates us spiritually to lower ourselves; it fills us with the happiness of life to become spiritually poor—this is the mesmerism of lust.

41. When you fall and master height—this is the peak.

It is apparent here that Nietzsche's 'higher man' weighs aesthetic delight with only one eye when even two eyes are not enough to see. In his snow-storm of happiness, bodily voluptuousness completely sinks his 'intellectual feelings.' So, with his innocent heart and symbolic happiness, Zarathustra descends deeper into his natural enjoyment to satisfy his *everlasting breath of passion* in relation to the polluted energy of the *pleasure principle.*

42. The free bodily instinct is the same *beast* that fights for existence.
As the equilibrium of the animal nature is in pleasure, an animal is excited towards pleasure by that animal part which is within it. For the freedom gained is the absorption of its passion, and in this enchantment, it gratifies its whim and finds its equilibrium.

Furthermore, once we enter into Zarathustra's garden of happiness, simple nakedness (according to his meditations) represents the essence of bliss: how could his very naked happiness be dressed afterwards by which sense? It is from the open window of Zarathustra's heart that in his garden of paradise it has been raining incessantly; his bare happiness cannot find any shelter, seeing that the bliss of his psychosexual naturalism is accompanied by the spiritual emptiness into which he falls.

43. An emptiness existing in the heart gives birth to the fall—into bodily pleasure without love.

Another question may be raised: what does sensual pleasure embody without the pure cognition to which Nietzsche pays such great respect; does it not simply cause disorder between the harmony of thought and the worth of beauty?

44. Delight in the glamour of the body does not mean love, if in this pleasurable charm is not disclosed the pure beauty moulded with the mind and soul, unrelated from free animal instinct. This is because love is defined with the value of pure thought, where such a definition is approximated to spiritual holiness; deprived of these sacred features the happiness gained becomes shorn of super loveliness and being married to passionate enchantment is fated to be debauched.

But my happiness should justify existence itself!
(Nietzsche, *Thus Spoke Zarathustra*, p. 43 §3)

45. The genuine misfortune is a human being's inability to perceive the misfortune.

If someone parades knowledge while he is in reality out of his depth, he is either enlightened in the darkness or merely mentally sick!

46. The one who is enlightened by the spiritual darkness in his knowledge, feels light itself as a philosophical conundrum.

47. The free human disposition to the sensibility of the *will to pleasure* in its enchanting self is a betrayal of the path to beauty.

It is with a yearning for the divine feeling in our spiritual action of prayer to the Lord Jesus Christ and confession that we grow in the greatness of love, ascending from the dust to immortality.

48. The emancipation from sins is that thorny happiness whereby the essence of beauty grows to be sensible.

49. Longing for the beauty of soul—this is the most precious, whatever exists between life and death.

I think it will be helpful here to bring in Nietzsche's cynicism regarding Greek art in his work *The Birth of Tragedy* to evaluate his wisdom once again.

The most accomplished, most beautiful, most universally envied race of mankind, those most capable of seducing us into life—they were ones who need tragedy. Or even more—art? What for?—Greek art?
(Nietzsche, *The Birth of Tragedy*, p. 3)

Tragedy is dead! Poetry itself died with it! (Ibid., 54)

In truth, Nietzsche's universally seductive art passed away with his sensitive poetry—but without tragedy or regret! The accuracy of Nietzsche's psychological analyses concerning the monkey side of man can be seen.

Once you were apes, and even now man is more of an ape than any ape.
(Nietzsche, Thus Spoke Zarathustra, p. 42)

Here Nietzsche penetrates deep into the satirical psyche in his skilful exposure of behavioural naturalists as hypocrites. However, in the same breath he attacks the pure feelings of human dignity, turning himself into the monkey he thought to mock, becoming a clown through his own efforts. Can 'the architect of morality' be a liar? In *Beyond Good and Evil*, Nietzsche calls attantion to:

...something in the morality of Plato, which does not really belong to Plato, but which only appears in his philosophy. (Nietzsche, *Beyond Good and Evil*, p. 56 §190)

And from Zarathustra:

I love him whose soul is lavish, who neither wants nor returns thanks:
for he always gives and will not preserve himself.
(Nietzsche, *Thus Spoke Zarathustra*, p. 44)

This is something in the spirituality of Nietzsche which does not really belong to Nietzsche, but which only appears in his philosophy—is it not? In this passage, generosity and kindness represent perfection for Nietzsche's animal instinct, who wants nothing for himself.?!

But how can the lavish and altruistic soul be achievable when supremacy is given to animal pride and instincts which are selfish in themselves, and upon which is built all Nietzsche's philosophical doctrine?—His empirical fantasy? With his hypocritical wisdom, Nietzsche bitterly lies once again. How can we bridge the gap between Nietzsche's apparently kind generosity and, for example, his later claim from *The Antichrist*:

What is bad? Everything stemming from weakness...The weak and failures should perish: first principle of our love of humanity. And they should be helped to do this. (Nietzsche, *The Antichrist*, p. 4 §2)

Where is that kindness which he professes to admire and love? Nietzsche shows himself in his true colours. But if Nietzsche only means Christianity here which is a week religion for him then why does he fight against it if he is spiritually strong and elevated? Apart from this, the meaning of this allegorical expression itself is the wicked interference in the cruelty of animal nature and animalistically demonized.

Not everybody can live like an animal and fight like an animal to be strong, and that which stems from weakness can be lovely as well.
(Shiolashvili, *Delusive Sensibility in* Nietzsche's Philosophy, pp. 20–21)

Evil is nothing but the going into self out of the immediacy of nature and is accordingly the first step in the direction of good. To be evil one must be conscious of the norms one rebels against and will ultimately obey. There is no element of chance in the going-into-self which leads to evil: it is the essential movement of self-consciousness. (Hegel, *The Phenomenology of Spirit*, §783)

Enough: for the time being belief in the body is still a stronger belief than belief in the mind; and anyone who wants to undermine it will most thoroughly be undermining—belief in the authority of the mind as well! ..."measured by intellectual standards, this whole phenomenon "body" is superior to our consciousness, our "mind"....
(Nietzsche, *Writings from the Late Notebooks*, pp. 28–9)

So how can Nietzsche's doctrine be interpreted? It might be said that it is better to be a healthy idiot than to be intelligent and sick. A philosophical dilemma, is it not? But let us define the case further: a smart person who is sick, in both cases, has an advantage over the healthy idiot. First, he is clever, and, second, to be sick is not the end. A chance still remains to succeed. As for the idiot, he will never become wise, and there is a high probability that one day he will become sick through his idiocy.

I would say that Nietzsche, with his bodily intellect, turns the value of life bottom up. If we share Nietzsche's idea that our physical body is superior to our consciousness, another question arises: is physical existence more vital than consciousness, as it would be with an animal? What meaning does bodily presence have without a notion of being human? The animal feeling as a matter in itself does not represent the notion, for it is empty, but the notion is transformed into feeling itself. Even as an atheist, Nietzsche's theory seems weak and regressive. It would be sensible if he equated awareness with the body as a whole. For example, as an atheist philosopher he could say: Belief in the body should be held on equal grounds, with the same strength, as belief in the conscious mind. Without consciousness bodily sensations are blind, despite possessing a natural justification in themselves. In this free animal blindness, their *will* cannot be ethical or true, only wickedly pleasing, defiling not only the subjugated mind but also the body.

Hence, anyone who affirms a priority of bodily purpose over the mind is subservient to animalism and perverts the soul. If Nietzsche meant physical survival as a priority of the body over consciousness in respect of animal functions such as eating, drinking, and satisfaction, then this is clear. We are aware that by the animal functions we into come physical being, but we do not need to pursue such functions as a vocation; this is not a kind of philosophy fit even non-philosophers. The gloominess of the matter is not that Nietzsche accentuates the importance of the body, but that his doctrine strives for the contrary side of the value of life. For him *an animal* is a *man*, and *a man is an animal.* The 'constructor' of our morality could not grasp that if you are a rational animal, this does not mean you are as yet a human being.

50. Without existence the value of life is absent—without the value of life, existence is non-existence.

51. The value of consciousness and the physical nature of the body are like two pearls of being in a human. The purer of the two is the most precious.

In Nietzsche's sensibility, we can still find a few truly sublime expressions.

For it is only as an aesthetic phenomenon that existence and the world are eternally justified. (Nietzsche, *The Birth of Tragedy,* p. 5)

On the other hand, Nietzsche's words do not represent a contradiction with other things he sought to apprehend, but merely a dualism he did not want to acknowledge: ascribing spiritual gifts to his animality mutilated the sublime world of his spirit and enslaved it to his worldly, covetous, and fallen self. Because of his animal ego, Nietzsche is thus shown up as an enemy of the eternal idea of beauty. His specific irritation also appears when he dwells on a Kantian interpretation of the 'thing-in-itself.'

The thing-in-itself is frozen to death almost everywhere.
(Nietzsche, *Ecce Homo,* p. 116, §1)

For Nietzsche, the original concept beautified by idealism drives humanity to degeneration (the illusion of comfortable beauty), as principles cannot be blended with organic sensibility in search of being exalted. Such imagery only resists the animal *free will* gifted by nature. There is no beautiful feeling outside animal passion that could be reborn inside—this is the misleading world in a person.

52. When the soul's beauty becomes visible, it exposes true love,
by which the divine wonder is eternally brilliant.

We must always remember that in Nietzsche's dictionary the word 'morality' is only a property of the gut feeling that we have to write off the spiritual consciousness. Nietzsche's ethical canon is expressed as follows:

I need to wash my hands after coming into contact with religious people.
(Nietzsche, *Ecce Homo,* p.144 §1)

Religion is a broad concept. Specified plainly, it is a branch of psychological pollution infected with superstitions and wicked convictions with a propensity towards violence. Yet, frustratingly for some, truth is personified in religion when revelation validates the truth of spiritual aesthetics, and the potential of its psychology authenticates the science of the soul. So, in this respect the washing of hands cannot be very helpful for the philosopher in any way, if his shaken brain is not cleansed as well. In his worldly self, Nietzsche was afflicted that the balance between the physical and metaphysical world is what creates the cultural core of spirituality, wherein self-admiration with its worldly glory bows to the mystery of the Word of the Deity, when the spiritual prelude of pure feeling conquers the eternal peak of beauty.

Do not give dogs what is holy, and do not throw your pearls before swine, lest they trample them underfoot and turn to attack you. (Matthew 7 : 6)

Do not think I came to bring peace upon the earth; I came to bring not peace but a sword. (Matthew 10: 34)

Accordingly, a battle conducted according to Christian rules does not reveal cowardice, but only selfless devotion to the value of truth; and nor does patience mean passiveness: sometimes, in view of its consequences, it is right to be more spiritually active.

For all who draw the sword will perish by the sword. (Matthew 26 : 52)

One should be warned, moreover, against taking these concepts of "pure" and "impure" too ponderously, or broadly, not to say symbolically. (Nietzsche, *On the Genealogy of Morals*, p. 6)

53. Without pure comprehension, a human being involuntarily becomes even more like an animal.

I love him who makes a predilection and a fate of his virtue; thus, for his virtue's sake he will live or not live. (Nietzsche, *Thus Spoke Zarathustra*, p. 44)

In Nietzsche's mouth, expressions such as *love, beauty, virtue,* and *morality* are demonic cheat. Through the power of the camouflaged evil lying between a human being and an animal, they become fascinating aspects of a merely physical reality. Hypocrisy is indeed a great talent of evil. What can be the virtue of an animal if not to take care of its own thick skin and be ready to die in the hunt for its quarry? This is its destiny! In Nietzsche's spiteful wisdom the notion of love is animalized within the proclivity of an intellectual animal. It is clear that Zarathustra's 'I love,' made out to appear sensibly beautiful, hides his hoggish constitution behind a more seductive and attractive aspects of caring, wherein the notion of love is foreign to his life experience of animal happiness, such as it is. Of course, we underline to the animal urge in a human being, but even if we close our eyes, it would nevertheless be impossible to imagine harmonizing love with the virtue of animal that is ready to die for its skin, or to live with its pride. This demonstrates that in Nietzsche's naturalistic self and malice, shrouded in Zarathustra's caress, there can only be the self-admiration of his 'intellectual animalism,' which is the ultimate source of his *free spirit*; Zarathustra again articulates himself in mixed demonic language, which reeks of his cunning eloquence. The word 'virtue' must be apprehended only as a simple tool of consciousness, and the only empire Zarathustra points to is his animal self-worth. In fact, animal functions are a million times more important for him, which raises the question: what must we die for? For the sake of animal functions or for the sake of *virtue*, which is only *a tool* for the animal functions? Nietzsche articulate the animal instincts as 'intellectual feelings' that do not need the *mind* for the survival of the skin. Here Nietzsche appears as a crooked conjurer who practices his skill before an audience in absolute darkness, so as not to be seen.

54. If the gloomy man delights only in the darkness, is not a delight also luminous for him?

Or in Nietzsche's naturalism, how can *a roe deer* resist the jaws of a *wolf* if its fate is to be weak in its beauty? Is it not the same happening in human life? Existence in this world is inseparable from sorrow and beauty. This is a pessimistic reality innate to the logic of the natural world, which is not admitted in Nietzsche's mischievous and deep-seated animal hunger—which blames the Christian world of an artificial longing for moaning.

So that, by the logic of Nietzsche's moral psychology of the *will to power*, *a roe deer* should metamorphose itself into *a wolf* and so become strong and save its life yet denying its tenderness and beauty. In other words, it is better to be like a brute in your power if you wish to save your life and live longer, than to be spiritually beautiful. A charming 'revaluation of all values!' Is not Nietzsche's hideous morality entirely anti-nature?

Learn to laugh to find your happiness—this is one of the main psychological doctrines for Nietzsche—but at the expense of what?

How much is still possible! So learn to laugh beyond yourselves!
Lift up your hearts, your fine dancers, high, higher! And don't forget
to laugh well! (Nietzsche, *Thus Spoke Zarathustra*, p. 306)

This laughter's crown, this rose-wreath crown: to you, my brothers, do I
throw this crown! I have canonized laughter; you higher Man learn—to laugh!
(Ibid., p. 305)

Can Nietzsche's crown of laughter be victorious in his moral psychology?

55. Sometimes joy is nothing but empty wind and the fallen leaves are the fruit of it.

56. When a mind does not embrace generosity, the thought which at once springs up in the frame of loveliness, receives an ugly face, and comes to be the possessor of joy.

By manipulating eastern philosophy with his decadent psyche, Nietzsche makes up his own supernatural science relating to the phenomenon of telepathy, which we might call Nietzschean 'empirical romanticism' by way of the metaphysical idea of 'eternal recurrence.' And indeed, he was forced to do so, since his nihilism was in need of a more convincing pillar for the validation of his animal truth. This means that by the *will* of nature everything is repeating, and that man will be reincarnated again on the earth with the same character and in the same moment, so that everything is calculated by Nietzsche—will then nothing be changed?!

This life as you now live it and have lived it, you will have to live once more and innumerable times more. (Nietzsche, *The Gay Science*, p. 341)

Unquestionably, the Nietzschean 'eternal recurrence' has also been pressed into service in the ideological quarrel with the Holy Scripture. It was perhaps Nietzsche's most potent psychoanalytic self-delusion to diminish *the pure world of mind* through the blind sensitiveness of the *will to power*, in his encouragement of joy over the fear of death. Does this mean that the one who suffered much and was tortured falsely will be sacrificed again at his next coming? Or that the one who maliciously obtained power and luxury in his life through the suffering of others will enjoy it again at his next coming? This is impressive justice from Mother Nature! Nietzsche spreads his *wings like an eagle*—however, he then proceeds to *peck* like a hen! To accept an idea, even as a theory, we need at least to determine the validity of the argument, what the motivation of this approach was, or from where it is derived. Nietzsche conflates Schopenhauer's *will to live* with his *will to power;* thereby seeking to convince us of his conventional truth of 'eternal recurrence.' Now let us see how Nietzsche *pecks!*

If time is infinite or creates an eternal circle of life, that is, if energy and motion participate with eternity to create this circle of life, then how can this eternal circle, energy, and motion exist eternally, if they are not real in-themselves? Here, Nietzsche is shamefully forced into using the Kantian diction he mocks, and thereby bows to Plato too. But if his formula of the eternal circle is not self-contained, but is dependent on something else, then how can this eternal circle be constant; and how can this energy and motion create an eternal circle of life by their own effort if they are dependent on something else? Here, as a sign of his wisdom, Nietzsche holds his tongue. Moreover, by by which mechanisms do time, energy, and motion create the *rational mind* in the living world if the *supernature of mind* is not revealed in them?

There is no account of this in Nietzsche's writings. Here we come across the same scientific vacuum in knowledge. The question is: if the *supernature of mind* is not revealed through nature itself, then how can it exist within us, if our life is derived from it, and dependent on it?—from which source? Pure logically, we have to deduce that the rational mind existing in the mineral body of human nature can be influenced only by the divine nature. This affirms the Kantian interpretation of 'the thing-in-itself' as the true concept. Accordingly, the thought compels us to assume that Nietzsche's theory of 'eternal recurrence' is based on the concept of the *will to live,* though his observation is defective and empirically illusive: it does not hold water.

As for Kant, the great error in his perception was his superficial attitude to the Christian idea. His transcendental aesthetics validated God as 'the thing-in-itself,' not only as a purely academic ambition but more as the knowledge and pure value of love within it, disclosing an eternal aspiration of the spirit, that is, that which cannot be perceived without the depth of the Christian psychology.

The beautiful is that which pleases universally, without a concept.
(Kant, *Critique of Judgment*, p. 40)

Even so, does this masterpiece yield enough sense to authenticate what is beautiful in its example of a flower? This maxim lacks universal validity and precision concerning the beautiful. A deficiency of synthesis between Kant's transcendental aesthetics and universal beauty is revealed, leaving us to conclude that it cannot be a perfectly fair judgment. The pure judgment in itself, upon which Kant formulates his universal validity, if it is perfectly genuine, ought to be canonized in the spiritual phenomenon of the Holy Word (Logos) in the supernature of Christ.

Given this, purity as the substance of judgment does not proceed either from the animal nature or a human being itself, but from the existence of God, in whom Kant himself believes. Otherwise, man's independent judgment would have at least equal status with the presence of God—but that is nonsense. Kant's intuitive perception and understanding of pure forms possess a one-sided view and are imperfect in light of Christian spirituality.

There is no moral law (pure law of the spirit) apart from that which is pure in its perfection, either transcendentally or empirically. In Kant's analysis of the beautiful, there is no parallelism between the comprehended beauty and its transcendental delineation of eternity that draws breath within the spirituality of the divine love, since he rests his judgment more on pure logic rather than the spiritual aesthetic he tries to persuade us of.

To attain the peak does not mean, as yet, to be on the summit and to touch anything is not the same as comprehending it. Kant's philosophy of aesthetic judgment seems to be aimed more at *things that exist in life than at the life itself in which these things exist.* It is disappointing that Kant's analytic critique can not be the universal aesthetic ideal either, but is only a reference of logical analysis in the service of immature philosophizing on this subject, bearing imperfect link with the eternal meaning of spiritual beauty within, which could disclose the eternal senses of the soul. A flower has no soul to estimate the beauty in its universal perfection. For this reason, pursuing Kant's thought, the sensation of beauty cannot be perfectly judged in the manner of the beauty of a flower even though it is a universal judgment. Therein, we lose an ability to discern perfection in the sense of the beautiful, insofar as the beauty of the flower is a modified example relating to the value of beauty in the nature of aesthetics, without including the human soul. Naturally, the inner beauty of man is unable to discern its true character in pleasure and its personality is predestined to be tempted into subjective blindness through its free attraction (temporary or partial fascination), which violates and deflowers the true nature of beauty in pleasure. The conclusion ought to be:

57. The beautiful is that which rouses purity in pleasure.

This kind of judgment can consequently be called universal, and only by expressing and discerning the pure word in the world of Christ can it be judged as the universal validity of beauty.

Red Rose, Simon Roman Kriheli, © Simon Roman Kriheli 1986

THE PRELUDE OF DIVINE WISDOM IN THE ART OF APHORISM

Philosopher, Simon Roman Kriheli, © Simon Roman Kriheli 2015

Another of Kant's arguments is the following:

This man is, then, alone of all objects in the world, susceptible of an Ideal of beauty; as it is only humanity in his person, as an intelligence, that is susceptible of the Ideal of perfection. (Kant, *Critique of Judgment*, p. 52)

Kant's idea of the moral law in pure aesthetic judgment is mistaken if it claims that the ideal of beauty is the property of God within us. Man is not the 'thing-in-itself,' other than in his dependency on mortal nature, and its natural substance can never be perfect in its judgment of an ideal of beauty. Therefore, Man's conscious mind always depends on subjective satisfaction in its natural imperfection of the spirit, and never attains an ideal perfection by its susceptibility to apprehend an ideal of beauty alone, it is only interrelated with God Who is in Himself. And alongside Kant's 'thing-in-itself,' Schopenhauer's interpretation completely fails to grasp the essence of the mode of the existence of God.

My body is the phenomenal form of my will; my will is the noumenal form of my body: my body is "appearance," my will "thing-in-itself." (Schopenhauer, *Essays and Aphorisms*, p. 21)

On the one hand, Schopenhauer here is close to spiritual truth, given that Jesus Christ said: *The kingdom of God is within you.* By defining the *will* as the 'thing-in-itself,' Schopenhauer highlights the eternal existence of being within the soul; in addition to that, he establishes his concept of the *will to live*. It is not clear what the true motive was for not allowing this purely philosophical idea to manifest in all its gravity—was it his self-admiration? As a philosopher, he should have understood that the *will to live* which is within us eternally, is contradicted by the disposition of our mortal nature. So, if both the *will to live* and our physical body are real, then in their essential contradiction there has to be a diversity of canons including morality, putting them under one secular law. For this reason, the mortal bodily self and its appetence cannot be prior to the definition of the eternal substance of being for the purposes of finding out the truth.

Following his claims, Schopenhauer's *The World as Will and Representation* comes to sound suspiciously like *The World as Schopenhauer's Will and Representation*.

The reason civilization is at its highest point among Christian peoples is not that Christianity is favourable to it but that Christianity is dead and no longer exercises much influence. (Schopenhauer, *Essays and Aphorisms*, p. 197)

This remark reminds us how Nietzsche acknowledges his debt to him.

Time and that perishability of all things existing in time that time itself brings about is simply the form under which the *will to live*, which as thing in itself is imperishable, reveals to itself the vanity of its striving. Time is that by virtue of which everything becomes nothingness in our hands and loses all real value. (Schopenhauer, *Essays and Aphorisms*, p. 51)

And concerning the path to salvation in the Christian religion:

They make their life intentionally as poor, hard, and empty of pleasure as possible, because they have their true and ultimate welfare in view. But fate and the course of things care for us better than we ourselves, for they frustrate on all sides our arrangements for an utopian life, the folly of which is evident enough from its brevity, uncertainty, and emptiness, and its conclusion by bitter death; they strew thorns upon thorns in our path, and meet us everywhere with healing sorrow, the panacea of our misery. (Schopenhauer, *The World as Will and Representation*, p. 466)

Schopenhauer's undoing is his equation of the idea of truth with the world of his personal will, logically driving him entirely to pessimism. He failed to distinguish true passionate love from worthless pleasure, wrapping them both in the same cloth of senselessness. That did not happen to him because of tragic fate, which has a rational motive for its existence within the cruelty of mortal life, something one should overcome. It is because of the rational synthesis with his 'will' not acknowledging the weight of the spiritual perception in the divine—namely, in the holy body of Christ. Schopenhauer's extraordinary gift fell victim to the self-admiration of his *world as will and idea*. A tragedy is always inevitable when consciousness is merely a tool for the physical body of a thinker.

58. The diadem of life amounts to the abyss of a tear.

59. The way leading to Christ is strewn with the thorns that adorn only roses.

60. A minute of desire fills the whole emptiness of the ruined past.

Finely, Kant's phenomenon is the great temptation of any philosopher who could not apprehend the spirit of the Logos. Inasmuch as the moral law equates to the pure doctrine of the soul, there is an indefinite distance between Kant's transcendental aesthetics and the transcendental aesthetics of the divine body. Kant failed to step into the kingdom of God to grasp the inner spiritual glory of 'the thing-in-itself,' erecting a one-sided philosophical monument instead.

61. Love in Christ embodies an indispensable condition of perception of true beauty.

62. The one who has discovered beauty a thousand-fold in the heart, has found that one amongst a thousand-fold.

What does Nietzsche think of beauty?

I want to learn more and more to see as necessary what is beautiful in things—then I shall become one of those who make things beautiful. (Nietzsche, *The Gay Science*, VI, p. 276)

But what Nietzsche had learned in his animal dissoluteness and slavery was the perversion of beauty through natural instincts. For beauty, comprehended or represented without idealism and purity, is a pity and depraved. Nietzsche's super hero Zarathustra, in the chapter *Intoxicated Song*, classifies the *will to live* within the project of 'eternal recurrence', as a part of a Nietzschean beauty.

Go but return! For all joy wants—eternity!
(Nietzsche, *Thus Spoke Zarathustra*, p. 332)

The real meaning of Zarathustra's philosophy is that the intoxicated man flays himself into an everlasting enjoyment of passion, till he is drunk or seduced and after that becomes sober again when returning to his mortality. Nietzsche reveals an old circle of knowledge, 'to be or not to be'—he find his solution in drunkenness and seduction, calling it 'to be!'

63. Stray sheep search for the shepherd!—Stray jackasses look for the jackass!

Illusoriness itself belongs to reality; it is a form of reality's being.
(Nietzsche, *Writings from the Late Notebooks*, p. 250)

Here I could not agree more!

In Nietzsche's philosophical heritage, however, nobody will be able to turn a blind eye to the master-stroke of his spiritual mood: *Without music, life would be a mistake.* This is a drop of pure aesthetic perception in Nietzsche's work, as if he almost surfaces from the swamp of his degenerate spirit, following the call of spiritual loveliness, but then all the same still forsakes it in his way of life, leaving his beautiful pearl an orphan, which remains very regrettable. His philosophy may yet pertain to metaphysical sensations of spiritual treasures, and this would indeed justify the *aesthetic phenomenon* of his life. Despite his disaster, Nietzsche does not change his route—it is biology that wastes and degrades all his spiritual treasures, in a way in which was not truthfully defined neither psychologically nor aesthetically in his phenomenology, blocked as he was by his arrogance and enslaved by lower animal greed in his self-consciousness. As a result, Nietzsche's philosophical psychology was destined to dive into the spiritual darkness to reach the bottom.

In *Thus Spoke Zarathustra*, which Nietzsche believed was the greatest wisdom that might be rewarded to humanity, his Zarathustra claims:

'Man is a rope fastened between animal and Superman, a rope over the abyss.'

This represents the Nietzschean mixture of biopsychology with metaphysics dressed with the face of an animal, a man, and superman. (The superman here is Nietzsche himself, who substitutes Christ for humanity in his life's work). Nonetheless, in this context, Nietzsche's metaphysics has only an external setting, the superman being a mere linguistic formula, as there is nothing super in his Zarathustra 'the higher man' other than his simply being an intellectually blind animal. This is not to deny that the book has a convinced creative style and brilliant sarcasm which gives it some deep philosophical vitality on its speculative depths. It is for this reason that this book remains psychologically addictive for immature thinkers and less experienced observers of the spiritual life.

However, from the phenomenology of the mind and its eternal values, a pall of spiritual futility fall over Nietzsche's bookish and sometimes plagiarized ideas, which are not related to his psychology, through which he manipulates. So, in my genuine perception and compassion—(although, in Nietzsche's animal ethic, compassion was one of the greatest disgraces for a man, as a real man in his spiritual battle must overcome his misfortune through his self-mastery alone)—all I can do philosophically is situate Nietzsche's reputation as somewhere between *a blind man* and *a clever idiot* in our cruel world. Nietzsche's perception may indeed be called into question using his own ingenuity: here drawing from the chapter of *The Vision and the Riddle,* where a dwarf calls Zarathustra 'the stone of wisdom:

Condemned by yourself and to your own stone-throwing: O Zarathustra, far indeed have you thrown your stone, but it will fall back upon you! (Nietzsche, *Thus Spoke Zarathustra,* p. 177 §1)

I would express this more precisely: *it will fall back upon your head!* The core of Nietzsche's philosophy is like the law of gravity: what goes up must come down, since no feeling or sense exists to transfigure it heavenwards. In his psychoanalytical empiricism, Zarathustra is Nietzsche's superman, like the 'sun' (the Nietzschean prototype of the divinity), descending to give light to humanity and in his modesty, wanting to be the man again. This is to sum up in a few words Zarathustra's portrait.

You have come up here to my cave for ten years: you would have grown weary of your light and of this journey, without me, my eagle and my serpent. (Nietzsche, *Thus Spoke Zarathustra,* p. 39 §1)

Bless the cup that wants to overflow, that the waters may flow golden from him, and bear the reflection of your joy over all the world! Behold! This cup wants to be empty again, and Zarathustra wants to be a man again. (Ibid.)

Zarathustra's portrait describes the eagle as a symbol of freedom, and a wise serpent as that of craftiness. Thus, when we are analysing Zarathustra's sagesity we should remember: *for a serpent, crawling counts the same as the flight of an eagle; but in the event of a serpent mastering oratory—such sermonizing is called snake-like wisdom.*

Throughout, with his literal and poetic astuteness, Zarathustra suffers from spiritual emptiness, even when his cup is full of gilded thoughts and enjoyment, and because of that our superman decided to become a usual man, seeking self-glory by his own down-going to proclaim the human superiority over the divine truth.

64. The spiritually fallen one is like a bottomless vessel, which is drenched with joy but never filled up.

65. Not only by its emptiness is that which is empty determined, for that which is earthly full can be empty as well.

Nietzsche's *Thus Spoke Zarathustra* is considered his most outspoken book, wherein he mocked the Christian religion. His philosophical technique is exposed in the metaphorical style of this literary work with some poetry, bearing witness to the uniqueness of Nietzsche's talent. However, his great rhetoric is destined to wither like a flower, as the truth of his philosophical fruit is rooted in the supremacy of bodily autonomy which can never be perfect in its self-determination, as it is based on the momentary completeness. In contrast, some parts of the spiritual gloom Nietzsche sees in the existing Christian study have a reality, concerning the superficiality of bookish priests. With his wording and artfulness, his Zarathustra is the most erudite hypocrite among them! in this fashion, his observation is genuinely respectable. In Zarathustra's disclosure, the moral virtue of humanity is represented by a beautiful warrior eagle flying above the abyss. From this view of wild nature, the Christian commandments are seen as feeble, drenched in slavery, counted as anti-nature and as the source of the degeneration of civilization. We may confirm that Christian self-denial and endurance reveal not personal cowardice, but rather a daily battle with divine rules for the immortality of the soul, which is indeed the question of freeing oneself from the *spiritual slavery of animal partiality.*

The value of life in the Christian world is not apprehended by the strength and achievement of a mountaineer when he climbs to the peak, but instead in the comprehension of love in the torment of spiritually, descending over the precipice to perceive its height.

66. The precipice filled by love captivates the peak.

What differentiates us from Nietzsche's *will to power* is our craving for the glory of spiritual love with the synthesis of physical love. *We aspire to natural strength for the spiritual value of the mind and we aspire to the spiritual value of the mind as well as for our natural strength.*

67. Is it not better to be in the precipice if by standing on the peak you are blinded?

68. It is not enough to spread your wings when you fly—it is needful to open an eye.

Even allowing that Zarathustra's metaphorical prose style retains a trace of the discernment of enjoyment of the vital nature, the pure intuition in his literary art is diminished by the sensitive illusion of the first impression of beautiful feelings, which in their fleshly language always reflect their dependence on the visual allure. Influenced by the sensitive and mutable instincts of the naturalistic liveliness, the human ego attains a kind of debased freedom through the act of spiritual falseness for the sake of a depraved happiness and its sensual joy. It is this which drugs the human spirit down to the slavery of partial instinct of animal nature through a *free will*, which perceives nothing but superficial beguilement, and it is this, in the depth of its craving, which results in ugliness.

It is not strength, but the duration of great sentiments that makes a great man. (Nietzsche, *Beyond Good and Evil,* p. 46)

Through these words, Nietzsche's analytical philosophy becomes embedded in an acceptance to fancy himself that afflicts the natural faculty of human feelings, which in their short scenario magnetize the spirit through their promised depth. It is that which makes sentiments great through its fleeting profoundness. Nietzsche's intuition is intended to glamorize the surface, since the eternal essence is not perceptible for him. Here is the way I will introduce great and enduring sentiments through spiritual deepness:

69. In the end, you will be forsaken, but even so, you treat them with mercy—this is mightiness.

He who attains his ideal, precisely thereby surpasses it. (Nietzsche, *Beyond Good and Evil,* p. 46)

It is applaudable, nonetheless, that in his nihilistic monism and literary flair, Nietzsche was incapable of perceiving the higher senses.

70. He who attains the unattainable creates the universal ideal.

Could Nietzsche, given the primacy of his self-will, experience spiritual ideals? Undeniably, it would paralyse the anatomical structures of his brain to give truly anything for love. That which concerns the satisfaction of the soul towards life does not accept the sense of its beauty under the dominance of pleasure as such, but only its pure rational supremacy over it, which constitutes its divine bliss leading us to the heavenly kingdom of immortality. Nor at this stage are we able to run from religious terminology; it appears as a demonic tendency in Nietzsche's sensitive idea of beauty for his psycho-physiological self-regulation by mocking idealism and divinity, crawling on the ground, and sniffing after paradise.

71. The snake which chuckles is more dangerous than the one that hisses.

72. Becoming a snake in a moment—this is humanly frightening.
Becoming a human being in a moment—this is the snake's greatest horror.

Nietzsche's profligate naturalism is found in his Zarathustra:

Everything falls away into failure, nothing falls any longer into deep wells. (Nietzsche, *Thus Spoke Zarathustra*, p. 204)

This seems a profound philosophical thought pertaining to the external living world, which in reality Nietzsche never follows to its essential truth and cannot in his animal naturalism. But the one who stands on the surface of his understanding may easily be tempted by Nietzsche's poetic charm to jump into his sensitive wells. There is an erudite duality in Nietzsche's cunning utterances, which sound as meaningful and deep, but habitually reveal his intellectual feelings to be spiritually untrue and self-delusional. And yet, what can Nietzsche's deep wells really be? His great skills in philology, psychology, and philosophy?—which are all encased in the materialism of the animal body, whereas surely an animal does not require faith, for it is indeed an animal. On the other hand, to fall into Nietzsche's wells depicts: humankind ought to be released from an understanding of 'sin' in order to overcome human affliction through the *free spirit* and 'master morality?!' Does any worthwhile meaning remain for our 'legendary philosopher? Could he have been woken from his intellectual animalism, his open-eyes sleep? Being released from the concept of 'sin' not the same as rejection of virtuous norms, separating the supreme acts of understanding and love from one another? After that, without love, what value can the notion have to fight in its rational deepness? Or how should love be treasured without the pure notion which reflects the inner beauty?—By the naturalism of the bodily self in its *free spirit* which psychologically admires depravity for its fleeting gratification to pervert the beauty of the soul?

73. Passion that cannot abide the pure feeling of the soul is as horrible as death.

The measure of *unbelief* of "freedom of the mind" that is admitted, as *an expression of the growth in power.* (Nietzsche, *Thus Spoke Zarathustra*, p. 204)

Nietzsche's lunacy knows no bounds. What sort of connection can be found between the *freedom of the mind* and the value of his philosophy when his mind is utterly governed either by free feelings or by animal favouritism under its slavish consciousness, whether he believes in something or not? Psychologically, a craving for power could facilitate mankind's wisdom, not self-indulgence, which thereafter develops rational darkness—this is the primary task. It should be noted that this is by no means a recent scientific discovery. So that Nietzsche's wicked speculation on spirituality reels around like an inebriate man, showing no other relationship between the *freedom of mind* and his predilection to power, blindly ploughing a spiritual path in his empirical psychology. Does the meaning of power have any value for the happiness of the mankind, if it disrespects the yearning of the conscious mind for dominance over physicality, from whence awakens spiritual values and belief? Is it not the same failure of humanity in the darkness to grasp the meaning of life, if the mind remains subservient, on bended knees, to the selfishness of the animal self-will? Does it not mean that the *freedom of mind* is to be like an animal with its powerful modes of expression, this being the very measure of unbelief? In such a union there can be no difference between the value of a notion and the animal urges that are the measure of unbelief—for which we can formulate only one word: 'evil.' With a pathological selfishness in his animal jolity, Nietzsche turns back the clock to the Dark Ages. However, has a bull in its ability of power more significance than the consciousness of a man?

74. A breast is not bared against a horned being but must be constrained to dance! (That is to say, the philosophy of the toreador)

This final, most abstruse, form of evil, whereby evil is perverted into good and good into evil, and consciousness, in being aware of its power to effect this perversion, is also made aware of itself as absolute, is the high-water mark of subjectivity at the level of morality; it is the form into which evil has blossomed in our present epoch, a result due to philosophy, i.e. to a shallowness of thought which has twisted a profound concept into this shape the name of philosophy. Just as it has arrogated to evil the name of good (Hegel, *The Philosophy of Right*,p. 139)

One more reality in Nietzsche's cunning and tragic nature:

When power grows gracious and descends into the visible:
I call such descending beauty. (Nietzsche, *Thus Spoke Zarathustra*, p. 141)

It seems that beauty is not tricky here for Nietzsche if we remember his admonition. We can see the reflection of two faces in this mirror: one that pretends to be beautiful, and one that is ugly but hidden. The beautiful face craves the phenomenological side of consciousness and experiences a sense of loveliness in the represented idea. Nonetheless, it descends into its subconsciousness, the conscious splendour comes gradually to be converted into an ugly spirit, dominated by its fondness for the animal self-admiration, which, for it is a million times worthier than the *beautiful states and heights of consciousness,* for its physicality is unable to be transfigured by the beauty comprehend in the individual who is whole and complete through *the word* of Christ. Our *clever idiot* could not observe, through his empirical science, that all beautiful states and heights of consciousness are one of the main guides for our physical perfection which is beyond animalism, within the mystery of Deity.

I am the living bread which came down from heaven. (John 6:51)

Truly, truly, I say to you...he who eats My Flesh and drinks My Blood has eternal life, and I will raise him up at the last day. (John 6:53-54)

The animal functions are, after all, in principle a million times more important than all beautiful states and heights of consciousness: these are a surplus, except where they have to be tools for the animal functions. (Nietzsche, *Writings from the Late Notebooks,* p. 214)

An additional observation on this metaphor is that Nietzsche thereby again deprecates the worth of aesthetic appearance in his philosophy, degenerating both the notion of beauty in man and the true nature of spiritual aesthetics. In this biopsychological statement, Nietzsche's emaciated perception uncovers a spiritual wretchedness as the result of his animal self-worth. Nietzsche tragically stands on the edge of nothingness and digs a hole in emptiness with his *animal wisdom of slave spirituality.* In the matter of temptation, the Christian religion reveals that evil is a con artist who metamorphoses his face into that of an angel so as to tempt the masses. From this revelation arises the question: did Nietzsche realize he had become evil? Nietzsche's phenomenology is another excellent example that turns Charles Darwin's hypothesis on its head. No man is descended from apes; instead, the ape is descended from man. Now observe how Nietzsche steals.

From the sun when it goes down, that superabundant star, I learned this: then, from inexhaustible riches it pours out gold into the sea—so that the poorest fisherman rows with golden oars! For once I saw this, and did not tire of weeping to see it. (Nietzsche, *Thus Spoke Zarathustra,* p. 216)

This striking portrait is written in truthful harmony with beauty, poverty compassion, and great love. It again articulates one of the spiritual principles seen throughout the Christian outlook, conflicting with Nietzsche's wicked and sardonic psychology. Nietzsche is forced to bow to the Christian psychology so as to describe his artistry with a true beauty of love in the tragedy of reality. A humble man is like the rainbow of life, predestined to suffer in his abandonment by the cruel world, and yet he remains humble in his love, which sticks in Nietzsche's throat for all the mocking compassion of his animal observation of the impulsive *will to power,* which without spiritual revelation is animalistic itself. Now look into his Zarathustra's cordial heart.

Alas, where in the world have there been greater follies than with the compassionate? And what in the world has caused more suffering than follies of the compassionate? (Nietzsche, *Thus Spoke Zarathustra*, p. 249)

In his inconsistency Nietzsche makes a fool either out of himself or others who follow him.

O my brothers, am I then cruel? But I say: that which is falling should also be pushed!..and him you do not teach to fly, teach—to fall faster!
(Nietzsche, *Thus Spoke Zarathustra*, p. 226)

But again, where here are his tears over that *poorest of fisherman*? If we compare the spirit of these two contradictory passages and truly believe they are written by one man, we should either accuse him of lying, or quietly call him a scoundrel. By this inconsistency Nietzsche confirms that his self is lost in wickedness—or that he is mentally ill, in which case my apologies to him! As for the qualities of the real artist, this is someone who can be merciless with himself, but not with others. Our great erudite philologist was not aware of this truth in his 'bread and art.'

75. Treat a swine humanely—it will smear you;
treat a swine as a swine—you will become like it.

Thus a man climbs on the dangerous pass in the highest mountain so as to mock at his fears and trembling knees. (Nietzsche, *The Will to Power*, p. 215)

76. Even the murkiness owns the peak, but man is like the precipice.
When he climbs to his desirable loftiness, he is happy—which is his destiny.

And once more, what should be the dangerous path and the highest mountain in Nietzsche's philosophical psychology? Rejection of the spiritual values for animal freedom or rejection of the spiritual values for slavish morality? In his instinctual freedom, Nietzsche speculates artistically once again, convincing us that to mock the fear of the eternal idea of God means as were being elevated above yourselves, which in truth serves Satan.

Or does it mean to overcome the fear of God is the same as mocking the fear of death? When you climb on the dangerous pass in the highest mountain by looking into the precipices your knees stop trembling? It is clear that Nietzsche's boasting to overcome the fear God on the dangerous pass cannot be valid either psychologically or spiritually. The psychological motivation of Nietzsche's *will to power* was therefore a contra-instinct of the sense of the fear whereto he was unconsciously subjugated. Thus, Nietzsche's heroic witticisms are false: they are glued together superficially by mere literary skill. Depending totally on his ego, Nietzsche was too gloomy to see the glory of beauty in the divine aesthetics, and in this case, naturally, the 'worldly truth' of his *will to power* cannot be ignored in the frame of self-preservation but only in human measures.

77. The wilder the man's spirit, the emptier it is.

78. To fear God is not cowardly but manifests one's own responsibility for the spirituality and supremacy of love.

79. The fear of God is a compulsory condition for the revelation of ethical virtue in human free will.

In his intellectual murkiness, Nietzsche believed he was the first to perceive the truth, the consequence and traces of which we might assume ultimately led him to the brothel. As an example of Nietzsche's eroded truths, Zarathustra proclaims:

In truth, man is a polluted river. One must be a sea, to receive a polluted river and not be defiled. (Nietzsche, *Thus Spoke Zarathustra,* p. 42)

80. An arrogant one is filthier than a swine!

It is all too apparent here that Nietzsche's Zarathustra, with the face of a goldfish, invites all idiots to swim with the tide in the sea of his wisdom, to be purified and persuaded that the *filthy* is *pure* and the *pure* stems from his superman's visceral and sensual views, wherein we can find the essence of life?!

81. A blockhead never grows old.

Sensual pleasure—but I will fence my thoughts around and my words too: so that swine and hot fanatics shall not break into my garden! (Nietzsche, *Thus Spoke Zarathustra*, p. 207)

Carnal pleasure attracts swine without love as well; accordingly, pure love has to be devoured in their piggishness to satisfy their sexual want. This raises the question: why does Zarathustra restrict his kind hospitality and ignores swine—because of his selfishness, or his blindness? I think, in this way, both are the same!

"To the pure are all things pure"—so speak the people. But I say to you: To the swine all things become swinish! (Nietzsche, *Thus Spoke Zarathustra,* p. 222)

I would add:

82. That which is swinish is pure to the swine.

83. A swine satiates with feed—the insatiable one insults a swine.

84. Those that are sated in the darkness die blind.

85. In spite of that, the symbol of the swine's freedom is dirt. Life is pleasant even for the swine.

When the seduced charm is turned into depraved satisfaction, happiness loses the worth of its sublime beauty; and therefore it loses the merit of its purity as well. Without purity even beauty loses its value, thus, without a pure impression the satisfied passion becomes empty again, as it loses its true spiritual meaning too. Such an aesthetic illustrates the Christian comprehension of human nature.

Why I am so wise? Nietzsche is afflicted by this question in his *Ecce Homo*. This is another symptom of our *clever idiot*. Yet altogether, I think we need psychiatric diagnosis here. (It could be that the symptoms of his chronic mental disease are less philosophical).

Nietzsche's influence on European culture is nothing but the confession of his words themselves:

In the midst of it a new transfiguring illusion is required if the animated world of individuation is to be kept alive. (Nietzsche, *The Birth of Tragedy*, p. 25)

Nietzsche looks into his aesthetic mirror and cannot recognize his own appearance. However, if Nietzsche had said *sometimes* the transfiguring illusion is required if the animated world of individualism is to be kept alive, the idea would be universal, but to Nietzsche's misfortune, all his spiritual truth was dependent on his animal psychology, leaving him in illusion, rendered blind so as to keep himself alive.

87. Sensitivity is seen as the attraction of glittering stones that hold dear much in their entrancing appearance, but they lose the value of treasure as their brightness is outshone by the awareness that their value as jewels is not real. That is to say, the illusion of appeal embodies sensitive blindness to its fascinating depth, always becoming exposed and devalued since it is comprehended purely semantically.

88. An ape can also see its face in a mirror, and this may not be considered to be monkeyshine, even for an ape. The real monkeyshine is when you see only your self and wish to judge another.

Malaise is conducive to introspection, and it was Freud's opinion that Nietzsche achieved a degree of introspection never achieved by anyone else, and never likely to be achieved again. (Hayman, *Nietzsche*, p. 1)

Absolutely, I would never wish anyone again to achieve the degree of our Nietzsche's introspection.

Convictions are more dangerous enemies of truth than lies.
(Nietzsche, *Human, All Too Human,* §483)

89. Is it not already blind self-conviction to believe only that which you see?

90. It is better to be fallen than to be made blind.

Untitled, Simon Roman Kriheli, © Simon Roman Kriheli 1984

Gelati Gospel, © National Agency for Cultural Heritage
Preservation of Georgia 2010

A Portrait in Aphorisms

A word is like a brush that paints a picture, and its creator tries to breathe
heart and soul into it, while simultaneously expressing the sounds of nature,
philosophy, music, etc. An aphorism is regarded then as a merging of art
and philosophy, the separation of which, one from the other, would leave
just small pieces, devaluing that eloquent picture intended to guide us
towards its truth. (Shiolashvili, Aphorisms, p. 7)

Or an aphorism can be characterized as being like a valuable stone. The purer
a stone is, the more precious; the same is the case with the thought. Thoughts
from the top of creation of art have to captivate us not only with the beauty
of their summits but with the depths of their precipices as well.
These are precipices that should be filled with the meaning of love.
For the purer the basis of thought is, the more brilliance its fruit will
display, and it is the brilliance of the colours of this very fruit that represent
philosophy. The fruit is its wisdom; the holiness its truth.

Embroidery of each word with the thread of the meaning of truth provides us
not only with a supply of importance to meditation but physically impacts our
sensibility, making us more pure and spiritual. In the inner self filled with the
image of divine thoughts, it sparks such a beauty that before it the full
brightness of materialism is seen to be worthless.

One of the main reasons for matter's formation is in the emptiness in which it
is yielded up, and without which it could not exist. So, it is that with the blend
of the matter and emptiness, physical existence springs up this is where the
thought builds its nest. If we recognize that this world embodies the little fruit of
cosmic energy in which the thought exists, how much more real is the existence
of such an element? And then the Questions: What is thought? From where has
it been originated? Through what kind of nature do human minds mediate ?

Philosophy is unimaginable without wisdom, or is it that wisdom could not be
imagined without philosophy? The essence of both is truth, and therefore their
indivisible correlation may only emphasize the true art of being. So,without the
revelation of true art into being, neither wisdom nor philosophy is imaginable.

With it, their spiritual harmony is like the perfume of that fascinating garden
of beauty that makes us drunk with the hope of eternity. And to be entirely sober
in such a garden is not only the negation of the true beauty
but a kind of blindness, too. (Ibid.)

Aphorisms

91. Life resembles a bitter tear that sparkles like a pearl.

92. Nothing is so utterly demolished and destroyed in this world—as when man is forsaken by God.

93. Even the sky fails to hold as many stars as a heart bears pain.

94. Life is but one—deaths are many.

95. When you stand in the sea of people and feel loneliness, the only reason is the blindness of their waves.

96. Lost time is the very same as untimely death.

97. Love is the soul's blazing fire, from which you burn when it disappears.

98. To fall in love with someone who cannot see your love—this is your true blindness.

99. Life is the sea of wonder—wisdom but a drop found.

100. The greater the height you conquer, the lower you stand; just because of this modesty the blind trample you.

101. Life kills more cruelly than death.

102. Every jester is an outcast in his own kingdom.

103. Abandonment by blockheads is not cause for commiseration.

104. Blasphemous contemplation like a muddy river flows as poison along its way.

105. Whoever breathes only air is a beast. (In the beginning was the Word and the Word was with God and the Word was God—John 1:1).

106. It is easy to liken a light-minded woman to a hen; to differentiate them from each other—this takes insight.

107. The future is the yoke for those who cannot see.

108. Nobody can say he is his own man, for every human being is destined to fall.

109. You have to swim through a sea of whore to achieve sanctity's shore.

110. Sometimes the heart's treasure turned into a stone is held more dearly than in the days when it had been treasure.

111. Whoever is able to prolong a second is a worthy owner of all time.

112. Even a tear of sadness may be turned into a tear of joy, but in its depth, the tear remains a tear.

113. The rock face of cruelty would be dried up from the bottom, if not for triumphant love made thirsty by longing for the height.

114. Buried and unconquerable is the one who fights in loneliness.

115. The body is the fruit of the ground—the word is the fruit of heaven.

116. Science is the body of thought; philosophy is the spirit of thought.

117. The divine hope looks like a rose springing up from a heart, which exhales the most precious fragrance of life.

Chapter 2

The Nietzschean World and the Christian Religion Today

Nebuchadnezzar, William Blake, © Tate London 2009

118. The more animalistic a man is, the more he is attracted to matter. The worldlier a man is, the emptier and more self-centered he becomes because of his gloominess.

We can see an example of this in Nietzsche's fallen nature.

And to repeat once more: the beast in us wants to be lied to—morality is a necessary lie. (Nietzsche, *Writings from the Late Notebooks,* p. 69)

All that we need to clarify is, which of them is the bully: the beast (the fallen angel), or morality within us? Nietzsche's disaster is that he is rationally obstructed from breathing loveliness into the *pure feeling of mind* within the Deity. As a result, Nietzsche's dissolute pride is forced into subjection to the lowest instincts of the flesh, for the sake of the vitalization of his spirit supporting animality contrary to the *beauty* of the *eternal feeling of the soul.* I would still rather have compassion towards him than laughter. So, the animal predisposition within us provides the fundamental orientation of the world's nature, but the genuine human ethos within us allows for the metaphysical thinking which is not derived from the real world. This is true up to a point: do we humans really exist physically in this world, or is this only our metaphysical conviction? Is this a scientific or philosophical failure in Nietzsche's brain cells? In both cases, Nietzsche's philosophical degeneration into moral vice is uncovered. What Nietzsche promulgated in his ethical revaluation was that to have animalistic desires does not mean immorality, but to resist this kind off fallen naturalism is regarded as anti-nature, (a dualism that causes unnatural suffering for the *free spirit*).

Nietzsche's defective linguistic cognition is also a broken bridge between phonology and phenomenology. Nietzsche's apperception and philosophy are entirely magnetized by the knowledge of biopsychology in its requirement just as it is, so as to rob and deprave the soul's beauty of man. It is true: a choice involves an instinct for its value, but an animal instinct itself does not include an option for freedom. It bears only a slavish attraction. Or should we promote the inner energy without the love which is within us? What persuades us that morality is a necessary lie and love can be true without it?!

119. The existence of consciousness as an inorganic substance in the physical body is caused by heaven. When its cosmological body turns into a tool, mainly, for the animalistic ego of man, a monster's appetite to subordinate the uppermost peaks of life under his feet is gradually awakened in his psyche.

In the animal world of animalistic liking, Nietzsche was invested with a similar title deed. From Nietzsche's legacy, the true essence of the Christian religion could be seen as tyranny over consciousness, education, and the whole idea of life, humiliating a man's will, forcing him to suffer by denying a true world for an illusive one. The latter, he believes, is to be overcome by his assertion of the *will to power,* which in spite of its master 'morality' is unable to heal brainlessness...

We have taken the fact that in order to prosper we have to be stable in our belief and made of it that the 'true' world is not one which changes and becomes but one which is. (Nietzsche, *Writings from the Late Notebooks,* p. 148)

Nietzsche even distorted the world as it is and could not awake from his degeneration within. Accordingly, together with Christianity, must we ignore theology, metaphysics, humaneness, idealism, the divine harmonies of great composers, and restrict ourselves to the spiritual virtues of mind with which we are privileged, and all the rest that humiliates and contradicts the naturalistic tendency of the animal world of Nietzsche?!

120. The one who keeps an eye on a stupid person is an astute observer, but the one who listens to him has already gone mad!

To all of these lauded wise men of the academic chairs, wisdom meant sleep without dreams: They knew no better meaning of life.
(Nietzsche, *Thus Spoke Zarathustra, Of the Chairs of Virtue*. p. 58)

Blessed are these drowsy men: for they shall soon drop off. (Ibid.)

By virtue of what does Nietzsche differ from these sleepers in chairs? Perhaps a great deal, but sleepers in sleep always look alike, and it is impossible to differentiate them by their actions, no matter that their reasons for sleeping may be different.

121. By freedom from natural instincts an animal will never become a slave, whereas the freedom of natural instincts of the animal in a human turns him into a beast, whereby he also becomes a slave of its animality, and therefore, consciousness enslaved by animal instinct is always drowsy in its meditation.

Our honesty, we free spirits—let us be careful, lest it becomes our vanity, our ornament and ostentation, our limitation, our stupidity! (Nietzsche, *Beyond Good and Evil*, p. § 226)

This is already Nietzsche's abnormality and the consequence of his philosophy with regards to the *slave morality of animal partiality in its own right*, which logically does not require honesty in its waking life. At the same time, I have to admit that in Nietzsche's early writings animalism was not a main figure of his philosophy, wherein can be seen a trace of some excellence of philosophical thinking, but his abnormal self-worship seemed to destine him to open the gate of his hell.

It follows that within the subjective satisfaction of animal instincts, we need to find our true self through clear perception of the negation of honesty measured by pure logic, that is, to recognise our spirituality stripped of honesty. In this fashion self-assessed pure logic represents a religious disease, and together with honesty, it represents a metaphysical virus to Nietzschean 'intellectual feeling' since it does not embrace animal naturalism in its *free will*, as the beast in us wants to be lied to—morality is a necessary lie.

122. A slavish soul is dirty like a swine.

123. Gloominess freezes the soul.

To sum up, Nietzsche's moral philosophy, the free spirit, functioning as the verbalization of feelings, is the *enslavement* of the *mind*. In the enslaved spirit, pleasure can be only slavish, whereas *the slavery* of *the mind* develops further animalism and its hunger in the rational nature. All these arguments allow us to conclude that the *enslavement of the rational mind* is Nietzsche's genuine spiritual freedom in his master morality. In conjunction with it, Nietzsche's free spirit logically falls into the psychological hedonism of animalism, while the psychological hedonism of animalism itself degrades the conscious mind in its craving for the highest goals. We have indeed inherited an extraordinary empirical truth from our *clever idiot.*

The truly great haters in world history have always been priests.
(Nietzsche, *On the Genealogy of Morals*, p. 7)

If a dull artist creates a painting, it does not mean the art itself has no value or spiritual attraction. When Nietzsche essentially attacks the genuine mission of a priests on historical grounds, he abuses not only Pharisees who deserve to be exposed in their materialism and parasitic life;—when from their red carpets, they sermonize to the indigent and barefoot people as to how they have to pass through the thorny way and be tolerant of terrible suffering?! That is to say; the concept of *divide and conquer* has been transformed in our epoch into the concept of *charm and enslave*—but Nietzsche essentially abuses the supernatural science of the soul. A genuine priest is seen as a nobleman in great love with human discernment, a guardian of the candlelight in darkness, a spiritual fighter and a follower of the pure culture of thought, as the other side of the coin. With his encyclopedic flowery language, Nietzsche can also be seen as a spiritual disaster, who as an intelligent idiot increased and indeed demanded our admiration towards animalism in the man spirit. Based on his empirical aesthetics, Nietzsche's philosophical psychology seeks nothing but to convince mankind that intellectuality and animalism grow from the same reason and craving. This could be said to be the basis of Nietzshce's spirituality. And now from the other shore of knowledge, that which is taken from Dawkins' *The Selfish Gene*:

Living organisms had existed on the earth, without ever knowing why, for over three thousand million years before the truth finally dawned on one of them. His name was Charles Darwin. (Dawkins, *The Selfish Gene*, p. 1)

124. A horned one and a blockhead look alike, but the dissimilarity is that a blockhead has the longer horns.

In The Selfish Gene, Dawkins tries to convince us of his pro-Darwinian theory of evolution, building up an evolutionary truth which is as defective as his cognitive awareness. In the second chapter, supporting 'natural selection,' Dawkins touches on atoms and chemical reactions, and for his final conclusion he enlightens us:

They are in you and me; they created us, body and mind; and their preservation is the ultimate rationale for our existence. They have come a long way, those replicators. Now they go by the name of genes, and we are their survival machines. (Dawkins, *The Selfish Gene*, p. 20)

Concerning the evolution of Homo sapiens, Dawkins' scientific evidence profoundly explores an animal that walks like a human with hands and legs but has no mind as we all understand it: Now they go by the name of genes... Dawkins never asks: by which substance are these genes programmed *rationally*: by which atoms? Carbon, hydrogen, calcium, phosphorus, sodium, iron, potassium, or...zinc?—Anything left? Do we need something more? Maybe they are rationally programmed within Darwinian selection's 'thing-in-itself' or the baboon's brain? On its scientific foundation, the explanation given by 'natural selection' for the evolution of Homo sapiens is partial and nonsensical, giving no supporting or cognitive evidence for the origin of the human spirit. Dawkins' empirical analysis plays a very malicious game with his primitive consciousness, insisting that God does not exist, whether or not we are happy with our personal lives.

125. Light is a miracle for the blind; for a being left in the darkness—it is always unbelievable.

126. The capability of meditation within us witnesses the real phenomenon through a miracle.

In truth, a gloomy morality does not emit light—with the same meaning the Chinese proverb is especially other way round here:

It is difficult to find a black cat in a dark room—especially if the cat is not there.

Yet in truth, we are left to wonder what more we could expect from a deluded man made bankrupt by his cognitive awareness in his spiritual disaster. Yet, that he should lecture us on moral values is miserable, even if some Christian authorities and Churches do give real cause for blasphemy.

Another atheistic intrigue:

As another aside, it has occurred to various people, including Robert Graves in his epic novel King Jesus, that poor Judas Iscariot has received a bad deal from history, given that his 'betrayal' was a necessary part of the cosmetic plan. The same could be said Jesus alleged murderers. If Jesus wanted to be betrayed and then murdered in order that he could redeem us all, isn't it rather unfair of those who consider themselves redeemed to take it out on Judas and on Jews down the ages? (Dawkins, *The God Delusion*, p. 252)

The betrayal of Jesus Christ does not represent a phenomenon of Judas' personality, but in Judas' personality is revealed the worldly ego of mankind, the inclination to sin—is that not clear? From this standpoint the betrayal of Jesus was inevitable. In this inevitability, God reveals eternal life through the death of Jesus Christ for our salvation, so that there was no other alternative. In judging what would have happened if Judas had not betrayed Jesus, we then must remove the predisposition to sin from the psychology of mankind, which signifies the reconstruction of the existence of the mortal world in the immortal one—is this not understandable? Dawkins' confusion is apparent in the following:

> If the argument of this chapter is accepted, the factual premise of religion —the God Hypothesis—is untenable. God almost certainly does not exist. This is main conclusion of the book so far. (Dawkins, *The God Delusion*, p. 158)

It is important to note that Dawkins still hesitates at this point, saying 'almost certainly'—but is it not certain anyway?

127. There are many discourses in the darkness, for the reason that nothing is visible.

128. It dawns not because of nightfall; rather, night falls because of dawn.

Hume was also a member of the circle that looked down on the Christian religion.

> I beg the limitations here made may be remarked, when I say, that a miracle can never be proved, so as to be the foundation of a system of religion. For I own, that otherwise, there may possibly be miracles, or violations of the usual course of nature, of such a kind as to admit of proof from human testimony; though, perhaps, it will be impossible to find any such in all the records of history. (Hume, *An Enquiry Concerning Human Understanding*, p. 127)

129. Life is a miracle already real. So, he who does not believe in miracles cannot perceive actual reality. This leads to the conclusion that the genuine reality is in the miracle.

130. Don't look if you want to see.

The striving toward phenomenology was present already in the wonderfully profound Cartesian fundamental considerations; then, again, in the psychologism of the Lockean school; Hume almost set foot upon its dominion, but with blinded eyes. (Husserl, *Ideas Pertaining to a Pure Phenomenology*, p.119)

Concerning the Christian miracle: This ceremony takes place in the Orthodox Church in Jerusalem on Easter Holy Sepulchre in a supernatural way. The appearance of the Holy Fire is an event which occurs every year in front of thousands of visual witnesses.

What does Nietzsche see?

Once I longed for happy bird-auspices: then you led an owl-monster across my path, an adverse sign. Alas, whither did my tender longings flee then? (Nietzsche, *Thus Spoke Zarathustra*, p. 134)

Once I vowed to renounce all disgust; then you transformed my kindred and neighbours into abscesses. Alas, whither did my noblest vow flee then? (Ibid.)

As a blind man, I once walked on blessed paths; then you threw filth in the blind man's path: and now the old footpath disgusts him. (Ibid.)

Did Nietzsche ever bear the burden of death and mockery for the sake of the beauty of the soul, which is higher than the human self? If Nietzsche had accrued valid spiritual treasure from his path and had not gone the way of his blind self-importance, then despite all suffering and humiliation he would have seen the only greatness within the supernature of Christ.

But small is the gate and narrow the way that leads to life, and only a few find it. (Matthew 7:14)

The route is a deadly battle of the spirit. On this path, you are eternally on the verge of death, and die alive a thousand times, and after that are reborn again in your suffering to fight over and over. All along the way, the burdens of mockery and misfortune are laden on your shoulders—as you realize your own madness in the web embroidered by walking snakes driven by the power of their materialism. At this point, the only means of your spiritual survival is to challenge with the hope of the world of Christ all acknowledged 'wise men' and authorities, by whom you have been loathed and doomed to death. *It is also the way* through the desert of darkness, where the precipices have no peaks; when you are shackled by evil at every turn and every spiritual fall, losing your hope, wishing for your death, but still yearning for the victory illuminated in the word of Christ. *It is also the way* where supersensitive beauty is being personified in you, as a consequence of your suffering. *It is also the way* when Christ indeed raises hope from your dead spiritual feelings and leads you to battle for the supreme victory. *It is also the way* where the forsaken and humiliated outcast becomes glorified within the immortality of divine beauty.

131. To walk the way of truth is more significant than to be born—to pass through this way is more bitter than death.

132. To be abandoned does not mean, as yet, that you are forgotten.

133. A martyr has a right to die—but not to be defeated.

134. Spiritual victory is greater than living, and stronger than death.

135. It is true the value of religion is always associated with the notion of purity, and purity with the uninvited guest of dirt, attached to it in its kingdom. Because spiritual purity personifies the treasure of beauty, and thus only in its sublime nature of the Word can the impurity of religion that threatens to triumph over the value of beauty be removed.

Inevitably, in the kingdom of moral values where the monarchy of the holy word is not acknowledged, its treasure is already corrupted and destined to be collapsed.

Holiness, itself just the set of symptoms of an impoverished, enervated, incurably corrupted body!...Christianity is based on the rancour of the sick, the instinct against healthy, against health. (Nietzsche, *The Antichrist*, p. 50)

...it has corrupted the reason of even the most spiritual natures by teaching people to see the highest spiritual values as sinful, as deceptive, as temptations. (Ibid., p. 5 §5)

Sensual pleasure, lust for power, selfishness: these three have hitherto been cursed the most and held in the worst and most unjust repute—these three I weigh well and humanly. (Nietzsche, *Thus Spoke Zarathustra*, p. 206)

136. How do you think? Can a jackass imitate a stupid person, even a little? No, but a stupid person looks very much like a jackass, doesn't he?

In my generosity I will uncover even more treasured wisdom:

137. A jackass by sitting on a jackass defines his height!

Moreover:..

138. The governor of a jackass is not the one which sits on the jackass, but the one who presides over the one sitting on the jackass! (This applies not only to a phenomenological aesthetics, but also to the political philosophy.)

With his antagonism towards spiritual loveliness, Nietzsche automatically sings a tune with the theory of the *pleasure principle* that is incompatible with the *pure feeling of mind* because of its lower instinctual penchant and egocentrism. Therefore, Nietzsche's philosophical psychology and empirical aesthetics support the separation between freedom and pure spiritual dignity that is supposedly needed for achieving happiness in our personalties.

So, in his philosophy, Nietzsche approves that the centre of physiology is the psyche, but it would be a great 'temptation' for his empirical science to analyse where the centre of the psyche may be. This is why it is only in an animalistic way Nietzsche should be accepted in his rights when he makes a laughing stock of the concept of sin with his polluted spirit, for the arrogant self-centeredness of his animal happiness was doomed never to recognize the true merit of love.

139. Men are born, become spiritually ugly, and then die.

The religion of the ethical Spirit is, however, its elevation above its real world, the withdrawal from its truth into the pure knowledge of self. (Hegel, *Phenomenology of Spirit*, p. 701)

The pure knowledge of self, according to Hegel, does not only mean the knowledge of spirit apart from the body, but it comes to know the worth of the body that represents complete knowledge of self.

140. The essence of the true word perfects not only our soul but also our body.

Christian philosophy tells us that the person is a complete individual substance, intellectual in nature and master of its actions. (Greenwood, *Modern Civilization and the Human Spirit*, p. 32)

Faith in the Christian religion is the model of true values. The phenomenon of Christian thought is the universal intelligence of the mind upon which depends the spiritual and sensible evolution of mankind, seen through the true nature of aesthetics, from the unconscious enlightened to the conscious mind.

Nietzsche blinded even scientifically to dress his animal intellectuality progressively, and his psychological observations are much too superficial when he claims that: Christianity is based on the rancour of the sick, the instinct against the healthy, against health. If cold water in winter threatens a human's health, it does not mean that the one who has tempered his body in cold water harms himself, but rather is somewhat healthier.

The Gospel is not a sweet garden of human *free will* but a barb within human sensibility which transfigures man's spirit into immortality.

The aesthetic comprehension of the Gospel and its pure dogmatic assimilation within modern reality is the wind of truth blowing through the wilderness, capturing the greatness of your love and elevating your soul to heaven.

When Nietzsche deserted the development of metaphysical values in his spirit, with his extraordinary narcissism, he should have been transformed into a rational blind animal. However, it was when he abused the immortality of God that he eventually became evil.

141. The feeling of the soul that never undergoes the loss of the loveliness of its height is pure. Hence, any treasure disclosed in artistic form can be true only through expression in the purest form. Distinctively, the revelation of true art in its attractiveness is always introduced to us with the unpolluted countenance of its elegance, for the sake of which the personification of its beauty in the material form demands acknowledgement of purity from physical nature. Consequently, only through the spiritual purity can the highest idea of aesthetics be discerned.

142. The revelation of beauty in nature with its pure form is kindness itself, for which it is beautiful. Likewise, kindness should also be pure to be beautiful, and it is love between their characters which grows into supersensible beauty that becomes supreme.

In the modern world, notions and attitudes concerning pure Christian dogma have divided, but if the Christian church represents the dogmatic body of truth in Christ, how can it be divided?

This is one of the bitter sides of reality expressed by Jung.

It may easily happen, therefore, that a Christian who believes in all the sacred figures is still undeveloped and unchanged in his inmost soul because he has 'all God outside' and does not experience him in the soul.
(Jung, *Psychology and Alchemy*, pp. 260, 261)

It is really a double truth, since Jung was outside of experience too. I will comment on this further in the next chapter.

143. Carnal lust is the demonic transformation of pure feelings.

Coveting the passions' spirited blissfulness for the glory of life, evil robs their heavenly attraction of its divine nature, metamorphosing that pure pleasurable sensation whose proper object is the achievement of the highest aim of happiness by the free spirit into the depraved gratification of animality; so as to enslave the bodily self through the fallen dimension of consciousness. From such an ecstatic height in conjunction with naturalism, through the involuntary function of the instincts, the passions see this filthy sensuality as the essential and paradisal in its rapture, which consequently yields to the feeling of disaster after self-gratification has run its course.

144. Holiness also adorns a stone whereby it sparkles, but whatever value it must bear, it remains surrounded by stone, nothing more than a fossil.
(This is their canonical externality when there is a stone in place of their hearts.)

145. Born of a Pharisee is half a monkey, half a snake.

When the church is politicized and involved with politics—politics should become pure like the church, otherwise, the church becomes as cunning as politics.

Spiritual corruption is a wave of unctuousness in the democratic approach to the holy shore of the Christian understanding by degeneration of the sublime sensibility in faith and God as it stands within immortality. 'The modernization of holiness'—even linguistically this has a cynical ring. Democracy is not the same as pure morality and will never be equated to it because of its worldly reason. There is no dispute that everybody must equally be given a democratic roof for the dwelling of their rights. However, not all democratic rights can be united with the divine values and morality, because the democracy of merely human *free will* cannot by any means be divine. Accordingly, this kind of union in one right can be only autocratic, which therefore necessitates a democratic separation from each other, avoiding any kind of intruder within the free choices of human ethics.

> Fair is foul, and foul is fair. Hover through the fog and filthy air.
> (Shakespeare, *Macbeth,* act 1 scene 1)

There are two kinds of laws, laws of nature and laws of right. (Hegel, 2015, xiii)

For this reason, God gave them up to degrading passions. Their women exchanged natural intercourse for unnatural, and in the same way also the men, giving up natural intercourse with women, were consumed with passion one for one another. Men committed shameless acts with men and received in their own persons the due penalty for their error. (Romans 1: 27)

Paul's words: for this reason God gave them up to degrading passions inform us that God has accepted the tragedy upon their unnatural intercourse.

The Political Invasion

> Jesus said to them, render to Caesar the things that are Caesar's and to God the things that are God's. And they were amazed at him. (Mark 12: 18)

With this answer, Christ revealed a balance between material and spirtual merit, which requires equilibrium to maintain peace. The imbalance and tension in the world today should be interpreted in terms of living values that which belongs to God is also rendered to Caesar.

> Thinkers make politics; it is not politics that makes the thinker.
> This in itself reveals that the essentials of thinking do not entail the existence of politics; the former's source is only partially associated with the latter's framework, which consequently portrays no more than an outward face of thinking in its materialism.

On this basis, we may take it as a matter of course that the creation of a sensible political system to avoid any deception within the definition of its real picture is, primarily, to master the intrinsic basis of thinking as related to the *pure essence of mind.* In point of fact, the existence of thinking itself is grounded on General Science and Humanities; yet it is the last which discloses the kernel of thought essential for human culture, governing the state and its priorities.

Characteristically, in the absence of the spiritual knowledge with a definition of *the eternal nature of the word,* which is rooted within the inner self of pure aesthetics, the psychology of a political picture tends to lead nations to cultural insufficiency.

Insofar as *political consciousness* in its positive frame-work inherits a merely outward face of intellectual thinking for the instinctive regulation and satisfaction of norms, all its authority in its picture-frame over the state and Humanities inevitably becomes subjective, and so insufficient to the core of thought and its aesthetic truth. Namely, *political consciousness* by its supreme jurisdiction of a self-portrait involuntarily becomes prejudiced against the *essential nature of mind.*

The national culture along with anthropology discloses its own spirituality, through which it embodies the genuine face of its sovereign state. Hence, when government policy likens the national ideology of its sovereign state to cultural liberalism and the credos of cultural heterogeneity as inscribed within a single legislative act, the political doctrine of the nation turns out to be an imprudent blend of Humanities and the incompatible tenets of religious psychology.

Therefore, the ratification of self-contradiction within cultural psychology authorized by political coequality cannot be approved without the perversion of language within human perception. Thus, deprived of the intrinsic truth and priority of its recognizable ethos, the spiritual and cultural identification of the nation loses its independence, and owing to the erosion of its national treasure, is predestined to be rooted out from its origin, and subsequently from the personification of the inner self of its kingdom.

146. Family institutions are not just bound up with sexual intercourse, but with the *spiritual* culture. *This culture* is related to moral virtues, whose roots of inner beauty are immutable because of their spiritual identities—otherwise, in family rights, we will not be able to avoid dissoluteness.

It has to be stressed that self-gratification as regards carnal pleasure, in the essence of a partnership, may not in all cases be dressed up with the concept of family and its rights. If the origin of its craving, and its passion, falsifies the physical genesis of human appearance; by which it degenerates the concept of the family as a whole and the spiritual appearance of the self within.

147. It is biopsychological naturalism in its charisma that coalesces pleasure and ugliness into one will. For the following reason, self-denial in the Christian religion should be seen as a step forward in the comprehension of truth.

148. To take communion with the eternal beauty of pure feeling—this is the essence of the whole Christian dogma.

149. Each nation that defines its spiritual self through merely political thinking, despite gaining every extravagance, nevertheless remains poor.

150. God is the true hope of truth.

Chapter 3

Political Model of the Will to Power

Socrates' Death, © Can Stock Photo Inc. / marzolinos 2014

From Spiritual Regress

You may have seen a long-necked hen passing herself off as a turkey; such political turkeys imagine themselves, head held high, in the starry sky; there are many who worship these illuminated, imaginative birds.

For those that are surrounded by apes:
beware of reward, and fear glorification most of all.

151. The jester's tears in his own kingdom amount to the state's downfall.

152. Where the value of a word is devalued it is impossible to differentiate the living from the dead.

153. It is not only a dog that gnaws a bone—so does an ownerless country!

154. An exhausted jackass is allowed a deep breath, then it is fed, and when it has eaten, renews its strength; afterwards it must carry its load and be governed again: such is the life of a jackass—so too a nation!

155. What do you think: does a free jackass have more need of an owner, than an owner has need of a jackass? If any of you say that they are equally dependent on each other, then who can say which the owner really is? Unfortunately, in a fooled country a human being has more need of a jackass; therefore, a jackass becomes the owner and the human being itself the jackass! Surely, in truth, a jackass should have more need of an owner—but next to a human being has to stand another human being, not a jackass!

156. A frog also jumps from place to place, and by that it does not betray its domain. But what sort of a man is it who will put himself in somebody else's place by jumping? A frog bears a name of its own, but it is nameless.

157. A jackass who is appointed to the post sings with the whole of his heart.

158. Sometimes even a jackass sits on a horse!

159. You search and cannot find, you eat and cannot be sated—this is spiritual darkness.

160. When jackasses are in council, a hound is howling all the time.

Towards Violence

It is better to face a monster with a head rather than a headless one,
as, if a monster is headless and still walking—it is more dangerous.

161. No whore can aspire to the betrayal which the slave to power achieves.

162. You're being throttled—even so they breathe through you.

163. For a worm that desires something rotten, is it not ripe for him?
Likewise, that which you accept as ripe is rotten.

164. The biggest swine among you is not the one that eats the most, but the one who rears such swine.

165. You intoxicate people with death, and when they sober up they are already buried. This is the insidious wine-maker who gives a joy to many for a minute.

166. You bury nation and retain your affluence—this is your prominence.

167. You cannot spare your soul for the sake of love, whereby your hunger for the crown of happiness is sated with the thorns of disaster, and, thirsting for beauty, you pluck roses in the garden of a grave.

168. Your value is as a rusty nail; power is the silvery hammer that cripples beauty.

169. Your eating is hunger; hunger—robbery; robbery—a tear coloured with blood, for which you sit satiated in your armchair: the tear is like meat to you.

170. Blood is being shed—you mourn for your power.
You are losing your power—you desire to shed blood.

171. You always eat what is rotten, and rotten you are!
Whatever man eats, he exists on indeed!

172. Mud is he who waits for recognition from swine!

It is obvious that the highest of spiritual values have unfortunately become otiose in many intellectuals, who daily cluster around the exterior comfort of a political consciousness increasingly plucked from Humanities that really needs to be epistemologically rebalanced in its political philosophy. In secular autonomy, the general policy has been spiritually emaciated and finally led astray, deprived of the divine morality which is key to the truthful prosperity of nation, seeking entertainments directed at decadence. It is focused on the superficial changeability of social marketing, in its perpetual dissatisfaction of pleasure and unavoidable greed. It is this which is isolated from the perception of *spiritual aesthetics* of the human self in many instances, which in the arrogance and comfort of government-industry has never been brought to the attention for the erudition of the political culture. And yet, is it worth arguing that *political consciousness* requires spiritual knowledge and analysis in order to balance the turmoil of the world? Following daily fashion, neither economic prosperity nor administrative stability will suspend the corrosion of self-awareness, leading mankind to psychological and cultural inanity by departing from the *pure aesthetics of mind and its spirituality*. So, all human knowledge and happiness come to be spiritually emptier in its sensibility, by that, more predestined to be tempted and captured by the charm of evil.

When political psychology is not accord with the pure theological argument, political consciousness falls into an internal conflict in its own structure, as it taints the spiritual constitution of human nature, as well as the core of spiritual aesthetics; the regulation of power in consciousness thus becoming chaotic itself, as it threatens a human's spirituality.

Philosophy cannot teach the state what it should be, but only how it, the ethical universe, is to be known. (Hegel, 2015, xx)

Philosophy at least cannot recognise the authority of feeling, inclination and caprice, when they are set in opposition to positive right and the laws. It is an accident, external to the nature of positive right, when force or tyranny becomes an element of it. (Hegel, 2015, xxv)

Aphorisms

173. The sage and the madman share a common trait: neither is concerned with anyone else's advice.

174. Earthly wealth is bounded by an empty frame; its unique picture is adorned with heavenly passions.

175. Being tortured for the sake of love: this is the hardest fasting and purification for your soul.

176. Going into the wilderness, one never comes back.

177. In search of truth you lose the pearl of your fate, so as to turn your very fate into the pearl.

178. Belief in Christ in His divine attraction is not fantasy, but rather the consequence of that reality, releasing us after all from every disaster.

179. If you cannot give your all for the sake of love—this is already betrayal, not love.

180. A hunter laments for a roe deer caught in a snare laid for a wolf—Is it because of the destiny which mediates between good and evil or for the offense to the hunter?

181. The happier man is, the more misfortune providence delivers him.

182. Who opens an eye finds it burns the hardest of all.

183. He who has received the sacrament of predestination alone has apprehended both his glory and death.

184. Man's life is unimaginable without a heart; so is a heart that is devoid of divine feeling lifeless.

Chapter 4

Nietzsche and Empiricists' Failure Concerning the Phenomenology of the Christian Religion

Gelati Gospel, © National Agency for Cultural Heritage
Preservation of Georgia 2010

Between Christian religion and philosophy, hostility, and more, can easily be found.

'I think therefore I am.'

Descartes attacks materialism remarkably acutely, and it will be tough to find any philosopher, artist, or intellectual thinker who is indifferent to this utterance—except, probably, first of all, Nietzsche, who must easily have been put out of sorts, thinking with his thick skin and not with his mind.

Unless one should make an exception in the case of Descartes, father of rationalism (and consequently grandfather of the revolution) who recognized only the authority of reason: but the reason is only a tool, and Descartes was superficial. (Nietzsche, *Beyond Good and Evil,* p. 191)

...there is no end to one's admiration for how the human body has become possible...For this 'miracle of miracles,' consciousness is just a 'tool' and nothing more. (Nietzsche, *Writings from the Late Notebooks*, p. 29)

Attractive Marxist nuances can recurrently be found in Nietzsche's biopsychology, as an intellectual philosopher and a founder of moral animalism. Thus, it can be acknowledged that the weight of two wrong-headed thinkers is less than that of one. So, the existence of the corporeal body in the physical world is the miracle of miracles, but does this mean that the existence of the incorporeal mind (consciousness) within it, is not a miracle? Indeed, even the greater miracle? It seems here that Nietzsche really became very off-colour in his clever idiocy.

To have a conscience, if conscience is only formal subjectivity, is simply to be on the verge of slipping into evil; in independent self-certainty, with its independence of knowledge and decision, both morality and evil have their common root. (Hegel, *Philosophy of Right*, p. 139)

185. Consciousness is the exposed mystery of life that remains covert.

186. The pure nature of true thought is the second breathing of life.

For Marx, metaphysical materialism in mind is also the product of a material organ, namely the brain. That is, the mind or consciousness is rooted within matter, and its substance derives only from its dependence. Let us follow the Marxist stream of thought for a minute. If the substance of the mind is derived solely from the naturalism of matter, then we need to synchronize the mind and matter, not only in their evolution but their decease as well, if they are produced from the same root. However, when the body (matter) ceases to function, and the digestive system within it is extinguished, the nature of the mind tries to resist death. It desires *to live,* which forces it to contradict the root of its synchronic perspective with the physical organs (matter). The question is: how? And why does the self-willed mind ignore the nature of the dying body from which it is wholly derived? From where does its disobedience arise, if it is rooted in the law of its mortal nature? It is a conflict of synchronicity that exists on a physical level and reveals the second nature of *mind* ingrained beyond the physical world, from whence its self-willed disobedience must, come, i.e. the *will to live.* Accordingly, the mind enters the physical world in two dimensions: the organic (mortal) and inorganic, the latter not belonging into the physical world in its origin.

187. A bonehead is determined by weight and not by the conscious mind.

A bit of the light of scientific observation is entrenched in the theory that our mind is 'an epiphenomenon of the body.' What does 'epiphenomenon of the body' mean? Is it a new religion, or scientific probability? The question here is: what is thought? By what substance does the mind meditate? We can ask: is morality simply a function of biology? How can we comprehend honesty through our sensory organs, with which animal substance? This must be a substance that is not included essentially in the visceral structure of a human or in the animal world but coexisting with its dualistic nature within.

How can conscience or morality be 'an epiphenomenon the physical body' alone which opposes the fundamental inclination of gut instinct in its pure dignity?—A contradictive dualism which is the essence of 'natural selection?' How could we develop honesty and a moral sense by 'natural selection' in the animal world without the spiritual substance of the *supermind*? The phenomenon of *free will* is enough to authorize it an origin distinct from the 'natural selection' of animal nature; otherwise, in one complete similarity, a free choice would be wholly subjugated under the roots of a free animal instinct and be deprived of the phenomenon of its *free will*, opposing the bodily instinct. That is, a free choice would have no possible space to develop from animal instinct: in its own space, the instinctive mechanisms in the constitution of the *gene* would have mutated it, demolishing its structure to gain *free choice*. That is, the rational mind could not bring into existence the self-owned body—that would be constituted by the rational mechanism and be dependent on an animal instinct alone. So, we have no option other than to acknowledge a dualist space in the *gene* for its growth, concatenating with the organic world of animal instinct and the inorganic world of a spiritual phenomenon in our physicality. For that reason, 'natural selection' for an animal species necessitates a separate space and diverse reasons for its origin and development, dependent only on the animal instinct of the *gene*. This leads us to affirm the holy world of the *supermind,* through which substance affected and magnetized the 'epiphenomenon of the body' with its chemical reactions in the brain, before which we can give an account of our sins.

188. The coexistence of cognitive awareness in the animal body is the phenomenon of the evolution of individualism with its consequences, wherein the human brain's apparatus is but a mediator between the organic and inorganic world.

Behind your thoughts and feelings, my brother, stands a mighty commander, an unknown sage—he is called self. He lives in your body, he is your body. There is more reason in your body than in your best wisdom. And who knows for what purpose your body requires precisely your best wisdom? (Nietzsche, *Thus Spoke Zarathustra*, p. 62)

189. A hopeless man grabs hold of the stream of his fallen feelings, succumbing to their lowermost.

190. There are pure forms imprinted in the soul worthy of suffering for its honour, by which tempering the spirit is granted the knowledge of eternal beauty.

The rational naturalism of a human, illustrating a passion originating from sensitivity to external beauty, is commonly changeable in its fascination, and all its bewitching allurement becomes impoverished when it attains the holy depth of cognition.

191. The truly lovely is only that; if even nearness cannot ruin its brilliancy.

192. When outward beauty does not embrace the depth of spiritual loveliness, physical glamour is defined by the blind human ego wherein it is charmed. Thus, if the sensuality of man is not accompanied by *the pure feeling of mind* within divinity, its allure remains on the surface of its enchantment—that is to say: there is emptiness in beauty. (Shiolashvili, *Delusive Sensibility in Nietzsche's Philosophy*, p.19)

193. The sole flaw of beauty is its superficial existence in human nature.

194. Only that who is drunk with spiritual beauty can stride in the virgin forest of wisdom.

For an animal passion is homogeneous with its disposition, which itself can not be exalted through the attraction of pure thought, as such a nature does not exist within it. Consequently, the animal has no wish or ability for self-denial: the true character of beauty would be nothing more than death for it (as it does not exist within it), and it is clearly easier to say 'God is dead' than *to die within yourself to comprehend it.*

Most assuredly I tell you, unless a grain of wheat falls to the earth and dies, it remains by itself alone. But if it dies, it bears much fruit. (John 12: 24)

195. You have to die in the word of Christ to comprehend true beauty—this is the only way to extricate yourself from spiritual emptiness.

196. The truth and the spiritual beauty are unrepeatable reflections of immortality.

In the same miserable manner, Jung sarcastically considers the existence of the idea of holiness in the holy ghost as manipulating the scientific postulations of alchemy, and expresses his mockery at the divine awareness externally. Let's look analytically at the defects in Jung's psychoanalysis wherein thought and consciousness are merely the products of chemical reactions in the brain.

In 'De sulphure' he says:

Thus the fire began to work upon the air and brought forth Sulphur. Then the air began to work upon the water and brought forth Mercurius. The water began to work upon the earth and brought forth Salt. But the earth, having nothing to work upon, brought forth, nothing, so the product remained within it. Therefore, only three principles were produced and the earth became the nurse and matrix of the others. From these three principals were produced male and female, the male obviously from Sulphur and Mercurius, and the female from Mercurius and Salt. (Jung, *The Conjunction*, pp. 288–9)

This means that the first source of aesthetic nature in the mind also comes from Sulphur, Mercurius, and Salt. It is clear that the mind is the only ground within a human being that strives towards scientific and aesthetic knowledge. Accordingly, the mind's longing for beauty should also be awakened by the nature of beauty. So, if the mind is the product of chemical reactions in the brain, then we may ask: can we discern the concept or nature of beauty within the knowledge of chemical reaction of the minerals Sulphur, Mercurius, and Salt themselves, or in the shape of the brain?

Does the knowledge of chemical reactions themselves in the brain express a beauty for which the aesthetic consciousness longs?..As we can find nothing within their knowledge and structure of chemical reactions themselves that would awaken the nature of beauty, the scientific theorizing that consciousness is just the product of chemical reactions should be acknowledged as partial and defective. If the mind derives only from chemical reactions that do not awaken beauty, then from where in consciousness is the yearning for beauty revealed, if its urge does not exist within it? This should mean that its motivation is beyond the world of chemical mixtures and experience, but is only disclosed through the chemical reaction which brings it into being, as animal does not crave beauty either. In the same way and action, a beautiful sculpture is conceived through the ideas of an artist. Accordingly, the chemical element in itself does not reveal beauty but it modulates the idea created by an artist, the spirit whereof beyond the chemical substance or minerals by which it is created.

The same thing happens with the chemical reactions revealed in nature. Their substances are only shaped and beautified by the sublime idea, which is beyond their chemical elements; otherwise, the minerals, Sulphur, Salt, and Mercurius would have the capability of meditation, being prior to the source of beauty and shapes revealed in nature; but that is absurd. Even if acknowledge that the origin of thought and consciousness is derived from chemical reactions, we still have to acknowledge the existence of two worlds: the material world for scientific definition, whereto is attached the human psychology, and the spiritual world, the supernatural, the phenomenon of longing for beauty, which is beyond scientific experience and apprehension. This means that Sulphur, Mercurius, and Salt are rational themselves and have the ability of thinking as the first source of the rational mind in nature, which is now doubly absurd. This leaves scientists in a huge, dark, psychological vacuum, confirming that there are two natures in one. This compels us to acknowledge the Holy Mind, the spiritual world of the Absolute.

197. The one is not one but two, but these two are not the same as one, but a different two, and that one which is truly one from these two, is eternal.

Anything a theologian thinks is true must be false.
(Nietzsche, *The Antichrist*, p. 9)

With a truly tragic delusion these theologians fail to see that it is not a matter of proving the existence of the light, but of blind people who do not know that their eyes could see. It is high time we realized that it is pointless to praise the light and preach if nobody can see it. It is much more needful to teach people the art of seeing. (Jung, *Psychology and Alchemy*, p. 262)

198. The existent darkness that cannot be seen by the eye is much gloomier than the visible darkness.

199. The mind's intercourse with hell is closer than death's.

200. *Free will* leads to human satisfaction but pure knowledge from the divine is mastery of love within it.

201. Christianity is the embodiment of the essence of beauty.

In contradistinction of that, pure or transcendental philosophy will become established, not as a science of matter of fact, but as a science of essences (as an eidetic' science); it will become established as a science which exclusively seeks to ascertain 'cognition of essences' and no matter of fact whatever. The relevant reduction which leads over from the psychological phenomena to the pure 'essence' or in the case of judgment thinking, from matter of fact ('empirical') universally to 'eidetic' universality, is the eidetic reduction. (Husserl, *Ideas Pertaining to a Pure Phenomenology*, p. 4)

In reality, our fundamental apprehension is sensitive through the instinctive nature with which we came into being and which represents our *first source of cognition*; in the craving of its natural truth, its keenness is rationalized within an instinctive sensibility that is aloof in time from the conceptualisation of the *mind,* as personified in our *second source of cognition* in time.

As a consequence, the vacuum in the spirit between the bodily sensitivity and the conceptualization of the *mind* becomes biopsychologically magnetized to the sensation of happiness determined by the sensitive partiality (our *first source of cognition*) which is a prior to our *second source of cognition* in time. That is, our *first source of cognition* is detached from the conceptualization of the *mind* in its first revelation.

So, we must recall that we came into being through the fundamental craving of the sensitive instinct of the unconscious, which represents our *first source of cognition* in time. This illustrates the essential destiny of one of the main reasons for the temptation of humans' *inherited will.*

Faith, revealed in the spiritual loveliness of the metaphysical world of Christ, is the revelation of infinity in the present time, wherein the worldly free will concedes its life's goal and aspiration because of the higher, for the glory of blissful eternity.

202. Obtaining the true harmony of the body and soul in its relations with the world requires their transmutation by that reason which comes from holy nature —for it is holiness only that embodies the soul's eternal existence articulated by the *supermind*, and through which it becomes possible to transfigure the temporary desire into the eternal senses.
(Shiolashvili, *Beauty is the Guide of Happiness*, p. 116)

203. The spiritual values symbolize the true face of physical sensations.

'What is true?'—The proof of 'pleasure' is a proof of 'pleasure,' nothing more.
(Nietzsche, *The Antichrist*, p. 50)

Nietzsche is again greatly submerged in his self-delusion—the sensation of delight has to be determined by the rational purity in the divine world in order to retain the inner beauty of the individual self within physical nature. This is the case because the glamour of bodily pleasure itself in its physiological hunger involuntarily mesmerises and seduces human psychology to descend to the level of a beast.

The evil within our spirit recasts the dimension of our aesthetic sensibility, the innate disposition to psychosexual affection in the conscious ego reverses the role of lowest into highest and metamorphoses foulness into pleasure, and disguises misfortune with happiness, which biopsychologically flows as natural.

Such is Nietzsche's approval of naturalism in his 'analytical universalism.' A spider sucking blood from a fly—this is proof of pleasure for it as well, but not for human beings. This obliges us to weigh the criterion of pleasure within satisfaction by personality's pure conscious self, not by the instinctive instance of biophysiologically motivated excitement, which can trap us in the web of hell. Hence the truth in pleasure should be determined not by its taste alone in our physicality, but rather by the pure apprehension of a personal duty within the divine nature.

204. Man's soul immanently characterizes its supernatural ambition for sensible purity in a heart—this is eternal; and if the physical yearning for completeness is not crowned by its sparkle, its adoring fascination comes to be filled with spite.

Compassion with the lower and the suffering as a measure of the height of the soul. (Nietzsche, *Writings from the Late Notebooks*, p. 150)

First of all, thanks Nietzsche for enlightening us that in suffering we are exalted we did not know?!—but the suffering for what? This is another of Nietzsche's diabolic analogies of spiritual ideas, the rephrasing of thoughts of which he has no phenomenological knowledge, intermingled with his empirical animality to exploit divine psychology for his own claimed originality. Or may we say that Nietzsche's animal caprice is worthy of mocking the spirit of Christianity? In this quote, the word soul, rephrased from the spiritual world, is just Nietzsche exercising false allurement. We have learned from the dictionary of his 'revaluation of all values' that the word soul indicates his animal ego, which defines animal freedom through *spiritual* and *moral slavery*. There is nothing else apart from it. I absolutely agree with Nietzsche that for the *will* of his animal ego, compassion should have a lower value; but alas, the measure of the suffering of the pleasure-seeker is his illness. It is unforgivable for 'the moral psychologist' to claim to know what he does not understand and to lie disgracefully in his misery.

205. To forgive a human—this is utmost kindness;
but to forgive the monkey—this kindness is superior.

"Let your love towards life be love towards your highest hope:
and let your highest hope be the highest idea of life!"
(Nietzsche, *Thus Spoke Zarathustra*, p.75)

This is one another a splendid quote from Nietzsche's rhetoric which in its poetic wisdom is mixed with emotional illusion. Nietzsche has a crafty analytical mind of his own and can be eloquent revealing the true merit in physical nature by being flamboyant, manipulating with the sublime world of man's spirit through the autonomy of his animal world by blending it with his visceral erudition, and sacrificing the highest feeling for the lowest instinct. This is the way of pragmatic naturalism for a brute—a brute that cannot sacrifice its self-will for sensible loveliness in order to be spiritually reborn in love, but sacrifices all that loveliness in whatever it touches in order to get pleasure and exist for the survival of its self. And let your highest hope be the highest idea of life —Nietzsche plays the wrong card. This is much too idealistic and transcendental for him; it is everything that he abhorred in his philosophy. What is the highest hope in Nietzsche's philosophy and where does it come from?—From the *spiritual slavery of his animality*? In Nietzsche's example, the hope, is unreservedly degenerated through the supremacy of the animal naturalism in its mortality which does not stand in need of faith?—and is this our *highest hope and highest idea of life*? Ironically and sadly, the impression he gives—how many times?—is of an idiotic cleverness, introducing himself through giving advice on the highest hope and the highest idea of life, as resituated within animality in his spiritually empty *will to power*. This is what gives Nietzsche his glib wisdom in his perpetually gloomy articulacy.

206. To concede everything for the sake of love— this is the divinity of beauty in the soul.

207. The value of hope is equal to immortality.

The reprehensible thing is that sometimes Nietzsche realizes that he is lying, embellishing his prose, drugging the conscious mind, arousing acceptance of deceitful stimuli and passion in its fundamental impulse to be trapped, as a jumping off point in support of his natural illusion. By this psychological method, he tries to challenge the divine values of spiritual truth, which aims at devastation of his ideology, threatening that his merely empirical optimism will come to naught.

Nietzsche is like a thief who disgracefully steals roses from a gorgeous garden into which he has sneaked, appropriating their enchanting blooms in his new role as the possessor of beauty. And then, he introduces himself as the wisest gardener through his tendentious rhetoric, and plants the heavenly essence of their beauty into the soil so to animalize it.

208. That which is animalistic is sweet for an animal; what is sweet for the animal is lovely for it.

The same meaning can be accorded to Nietzsche's great hero, Zarathustra, with his earthly garden of paradise, wherein his degenerated psychology grew. This is the superman who in his psychological empiricism is incapable of differentiating 'two' from 'one.' This is the superman who wages war against the honesty of the *word*. This is the superman who classifies spiritual values according to biological advantage and places the merit of feelings under the feet of animality, dishonouring the divine creative treasures.

Is it not a degradation of human psychology to bring into being healthy idiots? In this case, alas, I am forced to return to a thesis concerning the necessity of the animal nature and the value of the *mind*: what differences there may be between a *healthy* and a *clever idiot*, anyway? In respect of Nietzsche's empiricism regarding the animal functions and the *free spirit*, a *healthy idiot* could be *healthier* than a *clever idiot*. Let us nevertheless look into the sincerity of this question: why should a *clever idiot* be less *healthy* than *a healthy idiot*? Is he not an idiot as well? Hence, as stated by our great Nietzsche, it is not the Christian religion or theology, not idealism, not metaphysic but the *free will* in the animal naturalism that produces the vital values in self-consciousness for analytical judgment and cultural prosperity?!

Almost everything that we call 'high culture' is based upon the spiritualizing and intensifying of cruelty—this is my thesis. (Nietzsche, *Beyond Good and Evil*, p. 229)

Spiritualizing of cruelty—very impressive words if they did not resonate from within Nietzsche's psychological thesis. This is another of his lures and self-contradictions. Nietzsche makes a great show of his ignorance of the essence of the words he utilizes, bamboozling us all the way through. *Spiritualizing,* in his sense, means the impression of the instinctual blindness of free feelings, which testifies to the indignity in *spiritual slavery*, and he taints this word by using it. To unveil Nietzsche's charisma, and drag it from the indivisible darkness into light, I posit the following:

Almost everything that we call 'high culture' is based upon cultural animalism and intensifying of cruelty—this is my thesis.

In Nietzsche's case, when you plumb the depth and discover only the surface —this is called *primitiveness.*

Nietzsche's *flowery language* would only be a psychological pillar upholding his depleted world of the *spiritual slavery of animal partiality* and love of pleasure-seeking, even if it did not cry for the moon, and his mentality was not as profound as his linguistic fraud. We may also call Nietzsche a great thinker who emphasizes reality with one eye, whereas his second eye lies.

209. All that you can see is what you possess—the rest does not belong to you.

210. A human being separating himself from the beauty of the soul involuntarily becomes swine-like.

It is true that only an animal can be lovely as a wild beast, the attractiveness of which Nietzsche transforms into the human, to produce a higher animal in a disfigurement of the soul, turning over a new leaf—*I feel therefore I am.*

Chapter 5

Nietzsche's Metaphorical Collapse

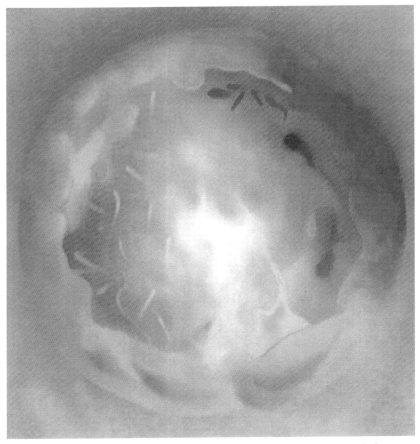

Seventh Sacred Round, Simon Roman Kriheli, © Simon Roman Kriheli 2014

What is bad?—Everything stemming from weakness. (Nietzsche, *The Antichrist*, p. 4§2

The weak and failures should perish: first principle of our love of humanity. And they should be helped to do this. (Ibid.)

What is the purpose of philosophy which seeks power and scorns beauty that is weak by nature? Is it a tragedy of the power or tragedy of philosophy?

211. Whosoever has partaken of communion with spiritual beauty has filled the emptiness of non-existence with life, the non-being of which bears the name of death.

"What is good—everything that enhances people's feeling of power, will to power, power itself." (Ibid.)

212. The beasts have their leader as well, but through that barbaric choice that is called brutality, and its essence is fear. (Is it not more frightening to be a beast?)

Nietzsche became self-lost again in his spiritual bankruptcy. His influence is really felt in authoritarian political philosophy and mobster psychology attacking with his horns and not with ideas. We run into an abnormal megalomania in Nietzsche's psyche, where there is an eagerness to fulfil man's ambition by fair means or foul. Or we may simply say: the *will to power* indicates nothing more than to get everything you want!—which is not philosophy even for animals, and not for idiots either!

This is another articulation of his mental hysteria, provoking a predisposition of fear veiled by death; Nietzsche suffers throughout his way, making him aggressive: the *will to power* should always be seen as the reasonable deduction from his animality, representing only a picked bone of wisdom that concerns fleshly preferences, not spiritual. We have already learned from his ethical eloquence: the first principle of love towards humanity. Nietzsche keeps going:

Not contentedness but more power; not peace, but war; not virtue, but prowess. (Nietzsche, *The Antichrist*, p. 4 §2)

Even if these words had been seen as a struggle with evil—how could evil have been overcome with more power? Surely the contra-action of evil with yet more power would have then come into play, seeking its self-preservation and survival in the face of attack? Where in all their power is the hierarchy of the mind in the definition of spiritual values?—Without which, good and evil come to be equated with the *will to power* and the right of survival. Once again, Nietzsche openly rejects spiritual values here: but war; not virtue, and longs for the *will to power* as evil that does not have anything in common either with philosophy or the one who claims to be a philosopher. It represents instead a total collapse of thought, even for a genius. From a different angle of Nietzsche's word, why should we not stand up against war if we search for wisdom in our mortal world? By this sentence, Nietzsche appeals even for bloodshed—but against whom? Against the canon of Christian spirituality, or for the subordination of mankind? This claim is more dictatorial than conceptual. Such a dictum encourages demonism, arising from Nietzsche's spiritual sickness, grounded in his frame of mind.

To be perfect in our judgment is simply a tyranny of thought, enlivened by a monster's appetite in Nietzsche's contradictive spirit, since God for him is dead and in his happiness, his bodily self becomes his mighty commander rooted in his empirical science. Two indispensable stipulations are revealed by the strength to exist in the animal world: *to be an animal, an animal has to live as an animal; to be a man, a man has to live as a man, not as an animal.*

213. The truth of the *will to power* is to long for the *eternity of beauty.*

214. Gaining love is the greatest revenge.

Can anything more powerful and worthy be imagined in the history of mankind's existence than sharing a glory with the eternity of beauty which is attracted to the divine?

Today I saw a sublime man, a solemn man, a penitent of the spirit: oh, how my soul laughed at his ugliness. With upraised breast and in the attitude of a man drawing in breath: thus he stood there, the sublime man, and silent hung with ugly truths, the booty of his hunt, and rich in torn clothes; many thorns too hung on him—but I saw no rose. As yet he has not learned laughter and beauty. This huntsman returned gloomy from the forest of knowledge. (Nietzsche, *Thus Spoke Zarathustra*, p. 139)

But the withered roses leave a greater pain than empty thorns—do they not? Seeing that Zarathustra never reflected on the sorrow of beauty, and his gloomy truth teaches us that laughing is to be happy, thus the ugliness of his crafty wisdom bears much more painful thorns than the prey of a disillusioned hunter.

Of all writings I love only that which is written with blood. Write with blood: and you will discover that blood is spirit. It is no easy thing to understand unfamiliar blood: I hate the reading idler. (Nietzsche, *Thus Spoke Zarathustra,* p. 67)

It should not be forgotten that in his incognizance Nietzsche too was writing with blood, and in his disaster, he could not foresee that some drops of his ideas allowed a barbaric fascist ideology to gain power. For blood without tears can not be accepted as human—nor blood with laughter…

"You shall not steal! You should not kill!"—Such words were once called holy; But I ask you: where have there ever been better thieves and killers in the world than such holy words have been? (Nietzsche, *Thus Spoke Zarathustra*, p. 219)

Is there not in all life itself—stealing and killing? And when such words were called holy was not truth itself—killed? Or was it a sermon of death that called holy that which contradicted and opposed all life? (Ibid.)

215. We should have empathy even with the monkey, for is it not a human too?

216. If you are involuntarily enforced to trample on a monkey, you are obliged to retain him human face.

Behold I am weary of my wisdom, like the bee that has gathered too much honey; I need hands outstretched to take it.
(Nietzsche, *Thus Spoke Zarathustra*, p. 39)

Woe to those…who put bitter for sweet and sweet for bitter. (Isaiah 5:20)

Nothing is beautiful, only people are beautiful: all aesthetics is based on this naiveté, this is its first truth. (Nietzsche, *The Antichrist*, p. 202 §20)

217. Nothing more beautiful than the word has ever been created—all aesthetics is based on this truth.

In the beginning was the Word and the Word was with God and the Word was God. (John 1: 1)

You look up when you desire to be exalted; and I look down, because I am exalted. Who among you can at the same time laugh and be exalted? He who climbs upon the highest mountains laughs at all tragedies, real or imaginary (Nietzsche, *Thus Spoke Zarathustra*, p. 68)

218. Even on the very mountain peak, a reptile chuckles maliciously and the fascinating beauty leans with grief against rocky slopes.

In the reality of this tragic performance, the sublime man prefers standing below in order to perceive beauty with a sense of grief, rather than to be like a reptile to which has been given the delight of creeping upwards to the peak, suffused with glee.

219. Victory does not reside in the presence of glee, but in the presence of beauty.

220. To comprehend the pure essence of beauty is to comprehend the perfectionism of joy, where the latter, in the sense of perception, is separated from perfectionism itself.

I name you three metamorphoses of the spirit: how the spirit shall be come a camel, and the camel a lion, and the lion at last a child.
(Nietzsche, *Thus Spoke Zarathustra*, p. 54)

What is heavy? Thus asked the weight-bearing spirit, thus it kneels down like the camel and wants to be well-laden. (Ibid.)

221. When the loveliness of holy thought begins to breathe into consciousness, man kneels in its beauty, acknowledging the truth of the supreme feeling of the soul which is within him. Because human pride and the carnal passion blemish the spirit, confession is the first step to an understanding of being exalted in love.

As to the snake-like:

222. A reptile cannot be made to genuflect—it has no knees.
(Though even amongst the kneeling can also be seen the likes of snakes)

223. The one who has never kneeled for the sake of love has never loved.

...or is it this? To feed upon the acorns and grass of knowledge and for the sake of truth to suffer hunger of the soul? (Nietzsche, *Thus Spoke Zarathustra*, p. 54)

Yes, it is true, one must suffer for the sake of truth, and it is not clear to whom or what Nietzsche complains:

224. You have to overcome a dog's life to go through all the steps of humaneness.

Did Nietzsche not know about this simple reality either?

But in the loneliest desert the second metamorphosis occurs: the spirit here becomes a lion; it wants to capture freedom and be lord in its own desert. (Nietzsche, *Thus Spoke Zarathustra*, p. 54)

But tell me, my brothers, what can the child do that even a lion cannot? Why must the preying lion still become a child? (Ibid., p. 55)

Under the circumstances I am obliged to shed some light on Nietzsche's meta-psychological drama in which *a camel* metamorphoses into a *lion* and the *lion* at last into a *child*—and what Nietzsche has swept under the carpet? Characteristically, until a *camel* becomes a *lion* it should first pass the way of a *jackass*! For when *a camel* ignores obedience to its own instincts it must appear to be as stubborn as a *jackass*. Further, if one day this *jackass* becomes a *lion*, it must really be a *super-jackass*! What, then, about this *foolish lion* afterwards? The *lion*, which has passed the way of a *jackass*, is twice as much of a *jackass*!

Now we need to get a *child* from a *lion*. If we look through the origin of this *lion*, genetically the *child* will have to be born with *big ears*, a *mane*, a *hump*, and at least a *short tail* and that is all. Such is the metaphorical fraud hidden in Nietzsche's three metamorphosis of the spirit, from *slavery* to *freedom* and from *freedom* to a new *era* of life. How *a camel* became *a jackass*, then a *super-jackass*—a *lion*, a *foolish lion*, finally, a *little monster*! This was all Nietzsche's metapsychological magic in its metamorphosis as regards the 'revaluation of all values' which was embodied in his *free spirit* I am afraid.

Can an ass be tragic?—Can someone be destroyed by a weight he cannot carry or throw off?...This is the case of the philosopher. (Nietzsche, *The Antichrist*, p. 11)

At last, we arrive at Nietzsche's honesty! Is it not better to be a *sheep*?

How miserable is a wise man who his whole life gallops on a horse,
only to find one day that this horse was merely a donkey!
(Shiolashvili, *Delusive Sensibility in Nietzsche's Philosophy*, pp. 19–20)

The chalk-line charmed the hen; the blow he struck charmed his simple
mind—I call this madness after the deed.
(Nietzsche, *Thus Spoke Zarathustra*, p. 66)

If only he could shake his head his burden would roll off: but who can shake
this head? (Ibid.)

Notwithstanding, Nietzsche's super-brain was well shaken, as he could not
realize that a *goose* pecks too, both philosophically as well as politically, and
there is no difference between the mind bearing the burden of a *real hen* and
a *goose*, even if the *goose* is philosophizing.

In the mountains the shortest route is from peak to peak, but for that you
must have long legs. Aphorisms should be peaks, and those to whom they are
spoken should be big and tall of stature.
(Nietzsche, *Thus Spoke Zarathustra*, p. 67)

Nietzsche's 'living wisdom' superciliously demonstrates his poetic illusion
once again. The shortest route cannot be attained from peak to peak, but the
precipice—because of which:

225. Every summit is exalted in loneliness.

Our superman's lame aphorisms were in accord with his cross-eyed vision,
derived from his brainless self-confidence loaded with his *will to power*. With
his philosophical eloquence and his long legs, Zarathustra turns out to be a
miserable turkey in the mirror of truth, like a proud cockerel looking down
on hens.

226. A cock that looks down on hens pecks just as hens do!

227. If you cannot bow, don't dream about height.

What is happiness?—The feeling that power is growing,
that some resistance has been overcome. (Nietzsche, *The Antichrist*, p. 2)

But did Nietzsche know the main purpose of this growing power in happiness?

228. Happiness is the true art of love.
(Shiolashvili, *Beauty is the Guide of Happiness*, p. 116)

What is great in man is that he is a bridge and not a goal;
what can be loved in man is that he is a going across and a down going.
(Nietzsche, *Thus Spoke Zarathustra*, p. 44)

The great in man is neither a bridge nor a goal—but the capability to comprehend the true word. Moreover, man is not elevated without a notion of the divine, which embraces the eternal loveliness within itself in either a going across or a down-going. As the concept of truth cannot exist without holiness, it is deflowered in time. What can be loved in a human is that which is sacred in his soul—that which is eternal and simultaneously exalted in beauty. Hence, *that which is sacred is truly lovable in its divine elevation.*

229. When the mind descends from the highest peak of beauty, it becomes capable of determining the higher over the defined one, of which the core personifies eternity.

This is *what* Zarathustra, (Nietzsche's higher man) in all his wisdom, did not mention.

And if one day my wisdom should desert me—ah, it loves to fly away!—May my pride fly with my folly! (Nietzsche, *Thus Spoke Zarathustra*, p. 53)

This is to say nothing in connection with *a jackass which speaks, and can even fly.* But if an idiot fortuitously predicts something, he really can be called *a clever idiot.* Despite Zarathustra's lack of belief in prediction, we can finally find a granule of bitter truth in these words. In addition, Nietzsche's animalistic inability to grasp the spiritual worth of thought in metaphysics or idealism compels him to cut off one of the important branches of philosophy. So, as he says, let his pride fly away—and then? What may happen to his sublime wisdom after all that?

230. Boneheads fly without wings—in the same circumstance, the wise prefer to walk.

Eh, how our Nietzsche loved eternity!

…and only when you have all denied me will I return to you. (Nietzsche, T*hus Spoke Zarathustra*, p. 103)

Truly, with other eyes, my brothers, I shall then seek my lost ones; with another love I shall then love you. (Ibid.)

…even me?

Without further comment I bring down the curtain.

Nietzsche's philosophy breathes life into contradictions, showing him up as a professional con artist in terms of the highest spiritual values. In Nietzsche's 'revaluation of all values,' the idea of freedom rushes onwards to an ethical virtue, perverting rational beauty—as it must, in the light of his psychological immorality about the *free spirit*—and establishing a new era of the *slave morality of animal freedom* in the world of philosophy. However, we need to allow that in his manner of expression Nietzsche could be praised as history's most celebrated poetic artist of illusive truth.

231. Whoever puts freedom ahead of pure humaneness is the monkey!

Nietzsche's metaphors and linguistic aesthetics, with their openly combined animalistic mentality, are evoked by the naturalism of evil. Literature and poetry should be represented as branches of philosophical knowledge and wisdom, but without the spiritual purity of thought they can be true neither in awareness nor in physical aspiration, even if they are pleasurable and logical.

For the essential worth of passion does not lie in logic or in pleasure, but in purity, which is the treasure of beauty within the meaning of pleasure, physically and spiritually.

Nietzsche is introduced to us as the Antichrist, openly evil, suffering from the spiritual desolation of his hatred of holy values. Nietzsche's cynicism is a tragicomedy of reality, wherein he is exposed as the great satirist with the face of a *clever idiot*, who knows 'everything,' with regard to the heights of spiritual values. With his 'earthly wisdom' Nietzsche always *pecks* like a *hen* before the eternal idea of truth. As to the *cackle*, it is the language of a *hen* which looks down not because it is elevated, but because the existence of its philosophy is dependent on *pecking*, revealing its earthly wisdom, which is a bit narrower than a chalk-line, while *an arrogant hen* is called a *turkey*! Nietzsche's *will to power* is the exposition of his failure in his spiritual battle with idealism and Christianity, couched both philosophically and aesthetically in terms of his animal 'master morality'—which in reality is *a genuine slave morality of animal partiality in its own right*. Moreover, if Nietzsche ever psychologically analysed Newton's Third Law *that any force (action) on a system gives rise to an equal and opposite force(reaction)*, he would have comprehended purely philosophically that psychology of the *will to power* would have had no chance of gaining superiority over being, but that only the supernatural reason of *mind* can do so. Nietzsche, as the greatest master of the invisible darkness and as the foremost of *clever idiots*, the most seductive in his pleasure thinking in his encyclopedic knowledge of animal nature, is finally removed from the *eternal loveliness of true thoughts and feelings*: that is, deprived of the *eternal beauty of love*—in both his life and death.

232. Even the ugly may be beautiful if no one can see what ugliness is and vice versa. But that which is not ugly and which nobody can see that it is not ugly, might be neither beautiful nor ugly, for in this case there is less blindness. (Shiolashvili, *Delusive Sensibility in Nietzsche's Philosophy*, p. 21)

Who could be Nietzsche in this world where there is less blindness? (Ibid.)

233. An adored word in gloom is turned pale in light.

234. When abhorrence grows into compassion—this is the height.

235. A man is a man only in God.

Still Life, Simon Roman Kriheli, © Simon Roman Kriheli 1998

Aphorisms

236. Even though hope does not subsist physically, it is mightier than matter.

237. He who disregards Jesus Christ condemns the honour of his soul.

238. Not by death is abandonment defined, but by betrayal.

239. There is no disparity between your word being trampled upon and your heart being buried.

240. If man could imagine how horrible his animal requirements are, he would pass away with trembling.

241. If something rotten is only threatened by worms, it is due to decay, and not the existence of worms.

242. He who battles unceasingly until he goes insane has passed through all the boundaries of death.

243. Every heart hankers after the joy that dispels death—such joyfulness is called happiness.

244. It is the one misfortune of a martyr, to shed a tear or blood.

245. Thousands lament over you—this love is great;
you lament over thousands—this love is greater.

246. The tear dried is the gained treasure of a lost life.

247. You are not judged as fallen at the time of your fall, but when you feel the inability to struggle against yourself.

248. Before sacredness even life bowed its head.

249. The true winner is made known in the fight with providence.

250. A swine lies down in dirt by its own will; a genuine man, walking on his pathway can only be thrust into it. All who are made dirty are thus not swine.

251. Life bears the burden of death; for the half-dead,
there is neither life nor death.

252. Some nations fall spiritually because of slavery; some, because of freedom.

253. By gaining knowledge a blockhead becomes sillier.

254. The world of living is within the soul—the rest is residue.

255. It is better to be an unorthodox Christian, but human, than to be orthodox and brutish, because a human has more opportunity to become orthodox, than a brute human.

256. Beauty perceived divinely by the mind of a human being personifies the idea of happiness. (Shiolashvili, Beauty is the Guide of Happiness, p. 116)

King David, André Beauneveu, © Bibliothèque national de France 2010

257. If a fleeting minute were not encapsulated within the eternal dimension, it would not have existed down the centuries.

258. If a human being is born only to die after all, then the birth of a human being must be viewed as the cruellest punishment, and nature the worst malefactor. Since by its very existence it naturally has the sensation of love, life cannot be regarded as such a malefactor.

259. The pure goal of life is to be attained on the verge of death; and if you don't die alive on the path - you cannot be victorious.

260. When they persecute you—you are threatened; when they erode your sanity—this is the real authoritarianism.

261. When the palpitation of life is barred by death—even the death dies too.

262. Patience, all patience, and patience again—afterwards victory!

263. The greater the throes of the heart, the more profound and unfathomable it is.

264. Death expresses reality—life exposes miracle.

265. To be a Christian was before now the worth of your spiritual greatness.

266. In that country where donkeys are hailed as men, humans are regarded as donkeys!

267. The most suffered is that fool, similar to whom there is nobody wandering in the world.

268. Among one million insane, just one of them attains his desired goal.

269. The merciless battle unveils selflessness—to endure a relationship with blockheads necessitates becoming a hero.

270. A fool is a little quadrangular, a blockhead perfectly round.

271. In the captivity of sins you are fated to become conscious of what you are; in such affliction, the rejection of your own self-will yields up a sparkle of spiritual dignity.

272. Sometimes fighting alone is greater than victory itself.

273. Love of wisdom is sharing the seen beauty.

274. To remain lonely with a tear is to be purified.

275. To attain childhood for the second time—this is already perfection in your spiritual wisdom.

276. A drop of love is able to cover a sea of sadness.

277. Life has its own heart, so one cannot be in communion with it through gluttony—it only pleads for the soul.

278. Prayer has to turn you into a child and not a slave, so as not to reduce your love before the Deity.

279. If the mind had the true cloth of human flesh, the mind would not be sacrificed for suffering.

280. The true sensation of love is in sensible madness.

281. The heart is as a laid table; the invited guest is empowered by choice—this is captivation.

282. Between the body and the depth of the soul is an indefinable boundary such as that which lies between earth and heaven.

283. Faith lost is like a rolling boulder crashing to the ground.

284. A seeker of love becomes lost in the sea of tears.

285. In spite of glaciations the peak does not lose its beauty.

286. The idea of beauty is one of the main pillars of the value of life and philosophy. (Shiolashvili, *Beauty is the Guide of Happiness*, p. 115)

287. The breathing of a soul is its beauty.

288. To be drunk with the true word is to be truly sober.

289. The divine idea in art personifies the true performance engraved with the diadem of grandeur of the soul.

290. The ways of the living are mud-spattered; so, from the window of happiness, those who are swine-like always have more fortune.

291. A women much resembles a falsehood; thus, men are in love with them deeply; and of course, women themselves greatly admire falsehood, because of their similarity to it.

292. To give blockheads food for thought—it already surpasses wisdom; as to wisdom, we need to be particularly polite to jackasses!

293. In this world speaking monkeys have been offered a greater portion of joy, humans—more sorrow.

294. Even a gloomy being will disown a greedy one, but a greedy being will never abandon darkness.

295. The true conqueror is not the one who attacks adversaries, but the one who conquers them by abandonment.

296. Having knowledge of what is true and be even verbally passive, itself signifies the achievement of an opposite goal; namely, acting against the true knowledge that you know.

297. Happiness within the divine is the fulfilled beauty of the eternal instant, celebrating victory over the few remaining minutes in space and time. (Shiolashvili, *Beauty is the Guide of Happiness*, p. 116)

298. Fasting is intended for human beings and not for swine; even though a swine starves, it remains a swine.

299. If only an executioner of his own life would embroider the crown of dreams by daily suffering—this is the torment that becomes truly worthwhile.

300. When an eye is not permitted to shed a tear—this is called the deathly imprisonment of the soul.

301. If your only hope is being tossed about in the grave of the soul—this is loneliness.

302. Even as many days as pass, so are as many desires for life buried in your ruined heart—this is patience.

303. They will turn outstretched roses into empty thorns, and afterwards twist these thorns round your heart—this is betrayal.

304. It always tortures you, buries you in tears, but despite all, you are still living and have no desire to be parted from this anguish—this is loss.

305. God is only powerless before Himself because He is God.

306. The one who is devoted to love is the only goldsmith of a bitter fate.

307. He who is driven crazy by life sometimes exhibits so much love that it is all the same to him, whether he speaks to the dead or the living.

308. To stumble on a human being with a pure heart is to find water in the desert.

309. They are the very same, human free will and misfortune, if in this freedom is not revealed the world of divinity.

310. It is better to fall blind, than to get on your feet blindly.

311. The greatness of a man is often comparable to dust whirled away by the wind, about to be thrown into his eyes, blinding him.

312. If a human being is born only to die after all, then the merit of the mind has no value at all.

313. You have given away nothing—and have thus not obtained anything. You have not conceded anything—thus you have understood nothing.

314. In the gloomy encirclement, the only way to survive is to convert yourself into a fool, so as not to go mad.

315. Devaluation of the word results in the ending of humanity.

316. You are in adversity when you beg; you are a beggar when you are unable to give anything away.

317. The virtuous man is he who strives for the peak, and on reaching it moves towards immortality.

318. The one who has fallen for the sake of love stands more steadily than he who has never fallen.

319. Love, all love, and still love.

320. If you have the ability to look all humiliation in the face, even though you are covered with soil, you have to reach whatever you see, which represents your spiritual mission.

321. Days leave nothing without response.

322. Love stormed from the waves of the past will demolish the hatred of eons.

323. The only value of life is in love, whilst the only value of love is in its immortality.

324. Through the thought, a fragment of matter and emptiness is personified; in its true essence, it is thought in itself, and there is left within it no trace of either matter or emptiness.

325. Thought makes sense by its immortality.

326. Everyone will receive the sacrament with death; just a handful, with life.

327. Roses plucked from heaven never wither.

Pieta, Simon Roman Kriheli, © Simon Roman Kriheli 2003

THE PRELUDE OF DIVINE WISDOM IN THE ART OF APHORISM

Bibliography

———. Augustine, Saint, Bishop of Hippo. De Civitate Dei [*The city of God against the pagans*]. Cambridge, MA: Harvard university Press, 1960.

Dawkins, Richard. *The God Delusion*. London: Bantam Press, 2006.

———. *The Selfish Gene*. Oxford: Oxford University Press, 2009.

Freud, Sigmund. *Beyond the Pleasure Principle*, trans. James Strachey. New York: Liveright, 1950.

Greenwood, A. H. "Modern Civilisation and the Human Spirit (Individuality and Personality)." *The Philosopher* 88 (2000), pp. 32–3.

Hayman, Ronald. *Nietzsche: A Critical Life*. London: Weidenfeld and Nicolson, 1995.

Hegel, G. W. F. *The Phenomenology of Spirit*, trans. A. V. Miller. Oxford: Oxford University Press, 1977.

———. *The Philosophy of Right*, trans. T. M. Knox. oxford: Clarendon Press, 1977.

Hume, David. *An Enquiry Concerning Human Understanding*, ed. l. A. Selby-Bigge. Oxford: Oxford University Press, 1902.

———. *A Treatise of Human Nature*, ed. Ernest C. Mossner. London: Penguin, 1985.

Husserl, Edmund. *Ideas Pertaining to a Pure Phenomenology and to a Phenomenological Philosophy: First Book—Introduction to a Pure Phenomenology*, trans. F. Kersten. The Hague: Martinus Nijhoff, 1983.

Jung, C. G. *The Essential Jung*, ed. Anthony Storr. London: Fontana, 1998.

Kant, Immanuel. *Critique of Judgment*, trans. J. H. Bernard. New York: Dover Publications, 2005.

———. *Critique of Practical Reason*, trans. Thomas Kingsmill Abbot. New York: Dover Publications, 2004.

———. Nietzsche, Friedrich. *The Antichrist, Ecce Homo, Twilight of the Idols, and Other Writings*, ed. Aaron Ridley and Judith Norman, trans. Judith Norman. Cambridge: Cambridge university Press, 2006.

———. *Beyond Good and Evil: Prelude to a Philosophy of the Future*, trans. Helen Zimmern. New York: Dover Publications, 1977.

———. *The Birth of Tragedy: Out of the Spirit of Music*, ed. Michael Tanner, trans. Shaun Whiteside. London: Penguin, 2003.

———. *The Gay Science*, trans. Walter Kaufmann. New York: Vintage Books, 1974.

———. *Human, All Too Human*, trans. Marion Fabber and Stephen Lehmann. St Ives: Penguin, 1994.

———. *On the Genealogy of Morals, and Ecce Homo*, trans. Walter Kaufmann and R. J. Hollingdale. New York: Vintage Books, 1967.

———. *Thus Spoke Zarathustra: A Book for All and None*, trans. R. J. Hollingdale. London: Penguin, 2003.

———. *Writings from the Late Notebooks*, ed. Rüdiger Bittner, trans. Kate Sturge. Cambridge: Cambridge University Press, 2003.

———. "The Will to Power," in *A Nietzsche Reader*, trans. R. J. Hollingdale. London: Penguin, 1977.

Schopenhauer, Arthur. *Essays and Aphorisms*, selected and trans. R. J. Hollingdale. London: Penguin, 2004.

———. *The World as Will and Representation*, 3 vols., trans. R. B. Haldane and J. Kemp. London: Sonnenschein, 1907.

———. Shand, John. *Philosophy and Philosophers*. Guildford and King's Lynn: UCL Press, 1993.

———. Shiolashvili, Zura. "Aphorisms in Lyric: A Christian Sense in Philosophy." *The Philosopher* 89(2) (2001), pp. 7–9.

———. "Beauty is the Guide of Happiness," in *Essentials of Philosophy and Ethics*, ed. Martin Cohen. Hodder Arnold: London, 2006.

"Delusive Sensibility in Nietzsche's Philosophy." *The Philosopher* 95 (1) (2007), pp. 18–21.

———.Snowdon, Ruth. *Teach Yourself: The Key Ideas,* Freud. London: Hodder Education, 2006.

———. Georg Wilhelm Friedrich Hegel, Introduction, *The Philosophy of Rights,* trains. S.W. Diode, (New York, Dover Publication, 2015), xxv.

Georg Wilhelm Friedrich Hegel, *The Philosophy of Right,* trans. S.W. Dyde, (New York, Dover Publication, 2015), xx.

William Shakespeare, No Fear Shakespeare, Macbeth, Act1. Scene1. Available at: http://nfs.sparknotes.com/macbeth/page_2.html